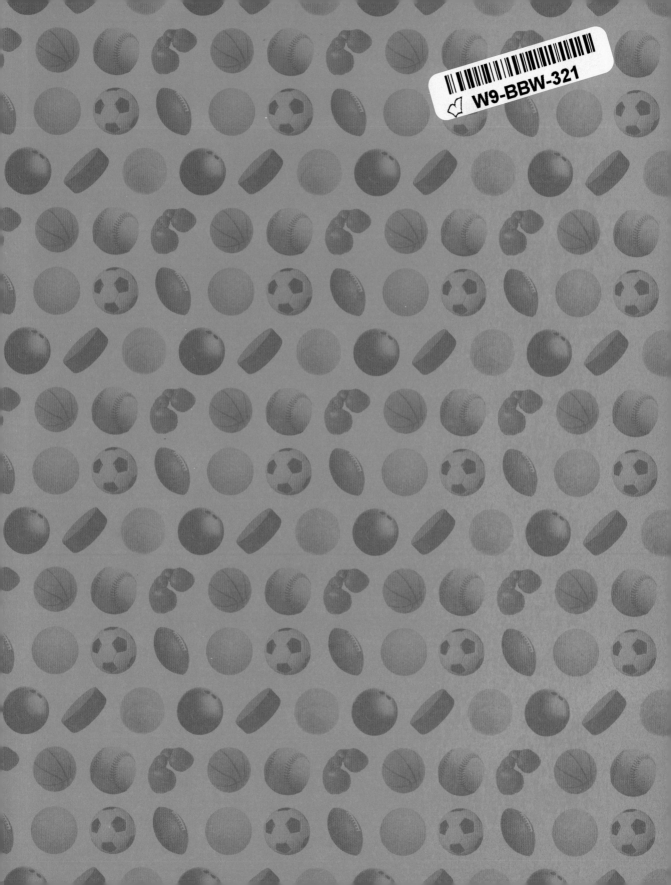

Popular Mechanics

WHY A CURVEBALL CURVES

THE INCREDIBLE SCIENCE OF SPORTS

PopularMechanics

WHY A CURVEBALL CURVES

THE INCREDIBLE SCIENCE OF SPORTS

edited by FRANK VIZARD

foreword by ROBERT LIPSYTE

HEARST BOOKS

New York

Contents

THE CONTRIBUTORS

THE SPECIALISTS

Matt Bahr: Kicker for six National Football League (NFL) teams between 1979 and 1995. He kicked the winning field goal in Super Bowl XXV as the New York Giants defeated the Buffalo Bills—the final score was 20–19.

Bob Bowman: Former Head coach for the University of Michigan swim team (2005–08). Bowman coached Olympic swimming great Michael Phelps to a record-setting 18 Olympic gold medals.

Buzz "The Shot Doctor" Braman: Shooting coach in the National Basketball Association (NBA) for more than ten years, working with such teams as the Philadelphia 76ers and the Orlando Magic. In the off-season, he runs shooting camps for players of all ages.

Peter Brancazio: Professor Emeritus of Physics, Brooklyn College, The City University of New York, and author of *Sport Science*.

Dean Golich and Craig Griffin: Coaches, Carmichael Training Systems, Colorado Springs, Colorado.

Jeff Huber: Former Head diving coach at the University of Nebraska and Indiana University and an Olympic diving coach in 2000, 2004, and 2008.

Jim Kaat: Major-league pitcher for 25 years, left-hander Kaat won 283 games and earned sixteen Gold Gloves while playing for the Washington Senators, Minnesota Twins, Chicago White Sox, Philadelphia Phillies, New York Yankees, and St. Louis Cardinals. He retired in 2006 after a second career as a baseball broadcaster for the YES Network and WCBS.

Lou Piniella: Former player for the Kansas City Royals, New York Yankees, Baltimore Orioles, and Cleveland Indians. He also managed the New York Yankees, Seattle Mariners, Cincinnati Reds, Tampa Bay Devil Rays, and Chicago Cubs.

Laura Stamm: Taught hockey players with the Los Angeles Kings, New York Rangers, New York Islanders, New Jersey Devils, and the U.S. Olympic team how to increase their skating speed. She is the author of *Power Skating* and operates skating clinics across the United States.

Dr. Joe Vigil: Legendary coach for distance running in track-and-field events and cross-country. His association with the U.S. Olympic team dates back to 1968. At the 2004 Olympic Games in Athens, Greece, he coached marathoner Deena Kastor to a Bronze Medal. He was named National Coach of the Year fourteen times and produced 425 All-Americans.

ADDITIONAL CONTRIBUTORS

A. A. Albelli
John Bakke
Stephen A. Booth
Davin Coburn
Wayne Coffey
Tom Colligan
Aubrey O. Cookman Jr.
John G. Falcioni
Steve Flink
Andrew Gaffney
David Gould
Amanda Green
Joe P. Hasler
Matt Higgins
William J. Hochswender
Alex Hutchinson
Miriam Kramer

Joe Lindsey
Allison T. McCann
Tim Newcomb
Charles Plueddeman
Steve Rousseau
Harry Sawyers
Allen St. John
Tyghe Trimble
Marita Vera
Ty Wenger

FOREWORD *by* ROBERT LIPSYTE

Science bored me in high school and scared me in college. But then around noon on April 16, 1962, in a dank clubhouse at the old Polo Grounds in New York, it suddenly became exciting and relevant. Jay Hook drew a diagram to show me why a curveball curves.

Not that I fully understood. I was a 24-year-old *New York Times* sportswriter and former English major. Hook was a 26-year-old right-handed pitcher for the New York Mets and an engineering graduate of Northwestern University. He was also a member of the American Rocket Society. The intricacies of Bernoulli's law, which he was explaining, were over my head. But Hook was a patient teacher and he was trying to distract himself; that day's game against Houston had been postponed by rain, and Hook would get the chance again the next day to register the very first win for what would be baseball's worst team.

He told me that the principles behind the curveball were the same as those that kept an airplane aloft. He talked about air pressure and boundary layers. "This is really quite simplified," he said apologetically. He was smiling when he said, "Just because you understand Bernoulli's law doesn't mean you can apply it effectively."

Hook was primarily a fastball pitcher, and his own curveball was hittable. He didn't win that next day, but a week later, in Pittsburgh, he did get credit for the first victory in Mets history. By that time, my story about him and Bernoulli, along with his diagram, had appeared and he was known in New York as the thinking fan's pitcher. I got more credit than I deserved for my science erudition.

But my interest was now piqued in the science of sports, which was just beginning to become an aspect of intelligent coverage of athletics. Over the next 40 years, we started writing about atmospheric conditions in yacht racing and the bone structure of racehorses. There were stories about the importance of the spiral to maintain stability in a long pass in football and about brain damage to boxers. The athletic version of the Cold War—the Olympic rivalry between the Soviet Union and the United States—put a spotlight on the emergence of sports medicine, from orthopedic repair to chemical performance enhancement.

I wish I had been more sophisticated about drugs in the 1970s. While I was aware of "greenies," the amphetamines that baseball players popped like candy, it was years before I realized the impact of steroids on football and track-and-field events. I can remember looking at all the "backne," those splashes of pimples on football players' shoulders and backs, and wondering if the equipment was chafing their skin. The few times I asked, I got nasty replies that would now be ascribed to 'roid rage.

By the 1980s, most professional and big-time college teams had psychologists, nutritionists, and weight-training specialists, along with more and more doctors with prescription pads. By the 1990s, the technology was NASA-grade, from hand-eye training machines at Olympic prep sites to the heart-and-lung monitors the bike racers wore. Every sportswriter needed to know as much about fast-twitch versus slow-twitch muscles as about the Curse of the Bambino.

Of course, by the 21st century, the Curse was part of the science story. Babe Ruth's single-season and career home run records were again broken, this time by players suspected of steroid use, and that became the focus of a larger discussion of performance enhancement in sports and in the larger society. Athletes were undergoing Lasik surgery to improve their eyesight, as well as complex regimens of supplements and injections of anesthesia before a game. Why was that different from men using Viagra and opera singers taking beta-blockers to overcome stage fright and school kids being dosed with candy-flavored meds to keep them calm and focused? Weren't steroids, human growth hormone, and EPO logical extensions? Was science leading us into a "post-human" era?

The chance to talk sports with chemists, biologists, physicists, and neurologists was fascinating, but sometimes depressing. Most of this was, after all, junkie science, the search for better ways to cheat through drugs. I yearned for something more positive, another shot of Bernoulli.

Then, around noon on January 14, 2001, in a garage outside Charlotte, North Carolina, I became as excited as I'd been back in the Polo Grounds almost 40 years earlier. I was doing research in preparation for covering NASCAR in my *New York Times* sports column, and a young mechanic, noting my interest, showed me a square piece of aluminum with holes. It was a so-called restrictor plate, placed between the carburetor and the intake manifold to reduce the flow of air and fuel into the engine's combustion chamber. It was used in super-speedway racing to reduce horsepower and speed. It had been mandated for safety, but many drivers thought that because it made passing more difficult, it led to closer racing and more crashes.

For me, it was Bernoulli time again; I didn't understand all the science, but it led me to find out more—about torque, fuel consumption, wind-tunnel testing, and the growing call for head and neck restraints. After covering NASCAR for several years, I wrote a novel for teenagers about stock car racing, *Yellow Flag*, which gave me an excuse to spend even more time in the garage and the pits, talking technology.

I wish I had had some version of this wonderful book to refer to through the past 40 years—enriching games, answering questions. I'm sending a copy to my first successful science teacher, Jay Hook, who went on to pitch in 160 games over eight big-league seasons from 1957 to 1964, winning 29 and losing 62 for the Cincinnati Reds and the Mets. He then went into industry before starting a third career as a professor at Northwestern. Several years ago, after retiring from academia, Jay asked me for a copy of that story I had written about him in 1962; he couldn't find it, and he wanted his grandchildren to know he wasn't just a science geek.

I sent him the story and we laughed about legendary manager Casey Stengel's comment about it, which all sports scientists should keep in mind. When Stengel read the story the next day, he shook his head and said, "If Hook could only do what he knows."

INTRODUCTION

The ancient Greeks and Romans played sports with gusto, and the modern human being is no less an enthusiast. But unlike sporting contests of yore, science and technology now play more prominent roles even in those sports that have seemingly remained unchanged. Behind the thrown ball and churning legs lie such scientific fields as fluid dynamics and biomechanics. Technology is critical for speed in cycling, protection in football, performance measurement in every sport, and so much more.

Why a Curveball Curves is designed for both the player and the fan. The player who understands the science and technology involved in sports is a better-prepared athlete. Likewise, the spectator can grasp more subtle nuances of competition and better appreciate the effort that goes into an individual sport. Here, practitioners of individual sports, whether they are athletes or coaches, examine the science in their game.

Why a Curveball Curves reflects the wide-ranging interest of POPULAR MECHANICS magazine and its editors in many different forms of athletics. Some of the stories have appeared in the magazine, while other essays were written for this book. But if POPULAR MECHANICS can be said to have a favorite sport, it would be baseball, as that game has received the most attention in its pages. The magazine has a long-lasting relationship with Jim Kaat, an ex-major-league pitcher and television broadcaster, who authored a number of essays that appear in this book. Likewise, physics Professor Peter Brancazio of Brooklyn College, author of a book called *Sport Science*, has served the magazine as a longtime scientific advisor regarding the spins and trajectories of baseballs, footballs, basketballs, and moving objects in general.

Other luminaries who have penned their own stories include the clutch football kicker Matt Bahr and baseball legend Lou Piniella. Coaches often offer insights that surpass those of the athlete. Dr. Joe Vigil brings 30 years of experience coaching the marathon, his most famous pupil being Deena Kastor, who won a Bronze Medal in the Athens Olympics in 2004 and continues to rack up distance-running awards around the globe. Likewise, Bob Bowman coached Olympic swimmer Michael Phelps to a trunkful of medals. Jeff Huber served as an Olympic diving coach in both 2000 and 2004. When the seasons change and water turns to ice, veteran skating coach Laura Stamm comes in and gets feet moving faster. These firsthand accounts are supplemented by journalists writing on a range of sports that includes bowling, boxing, hockey, skiing, soccer, and tennis. Equally important are reports on behind-the-scenes trends in training involving vision, hydration, and lactic acid, to name just a few. And a cautionary note is sounded regarding gene doping and its potential to threaten the integrity of all sports, much as illegal drug use did before it.

So, whether you are minutes away from competing as a player or moments away from watching your favorite team, *Why a Curveball Curves* will make you love sports even more—and may even make you a better athlete.

Frank Vizard
Editor

CHAPTER 1

Training

START
WITH THE
EYES

by STEPHEN A. BOOTH

SEE THE BALL, HIT THE BALL. THAT'S THE MANTRA COUNTLESS YOUNG ATHLETES HAVE HEARD FROM GENERATIONS OF COACHES. ALTHOUGH MOST TRAINING IN SPORTS INVOLVES PHYSICAL REGIMENS LIKE BATTING STANCE, OR MUSCULAR COORDINATION SUCH AS SHIFTING WEIGHT, EXPERTS NOW STRESS THE IMPORTANCE OF EXERCISING AND TRAINING ANOTHER SET OF ORGANS— THE EYES.

Much is made of what's called hand-eye coordination, and while it seems to come naturally to some people, the visual component is teachable and trainable—for adults as well as children. That's the message from authorities such as the American Optometric Association (AOA), as well as optometric specialists at sports training clinics such as the well-regarded Frozen Ropes baseball franchise. Their advice and training techniques can benefit those who play golf, tennis, soccer, hockey, and other sports besides baseball, although most research has focused on the latter.

"How many times have your players just missed catching a ball by inches?" asks Dr. Howard Bailey, a partner in Frozen Ropes' vision-training program. "Remember the great players who were not fleet of foot, but seemed to be in front of the balls hit to them. They got a jump on the ball, or to put it another way, they had fast recognition/release skills."

The body goes into motion only after it receives a visual cue from the eyes to the brain, says Bailey. "If a fielder has an 11.5-second speed in the 100-yard dash, he would gain 27 inches traveling 30 feet by reducing his recognition/release time by 25 percent. Imagine how this training would benefit base stealing, running down fly balls, or any other action that requires moving to a spot to complete a play."

IMPROVE YOUR VISION

Improving one's visual skills for sports begins with a visit to an optometrist for a thorough eye examination, the AOA advises. An optometrist with expertise in sports vision can not only prescribe the right eyeglasses or contact lenses, but also can design a vision therapy program for a specific sport.

There are several components in maximizing vision for sports. These include dynamic visual acuity, or the ability to see objects clearly when you or they are moving quickly. Visual concentration, the ability to screen out distractions and stay focused on a target, is also important. "When you commit an error on an easy ground ball or miss a short putt, it may be that you are distracted by things that are happening around you," the AOA says in its report on vision skills for sports. "Our eyes normally react to anything that happens in our field of vision ... spectators, other participants, and even the wind blowing leaves on an overhanging branch."

Eye tracking, the discipline of following objects with minimum head motion, is an ability that helps players stay balanced and react to situations quickly. Eye-hand-body coordination, a term that describes how the hands, feet, and muscles respond to the information gathered through the eyes, affects timing and body control. Visual memory, the ability to process and remember a fast-moving, complex picture of people and things, also aids in fast action. "The athlete with good visual memory always seems to be in the right place at the right time," notes the AOA.

Visualization is another technique that can help your performance, reports the AOA. This involves seeing yourself in your "mind's eye" while your eyes are actually seeing and concentrating on something else, usually the ball. Equally as important as visualization is peripheral vision, which focuses on seeing the action around you. Much of what happens in sports does not happen directly in front of you, so it's important to increase your ability to see action to the side without having to turn your head. Other important functions that can be learned or can be improved with training include visual reaction time and depth perception (also called stereo acuity). The former is the speed with which your brain interprets and reacts to an opponent's action—say, in returning a tennis serve. The latter concerns your ability to accurately and quickly judge the distance between you and other objects. If you consistently over- or underestimate the distance to your target, poor depth perception may be at fault.

ADJUSTING YOUR VISUAL MECHANICS

Just as baseball players can make mechanical adjustments to their swing, it's possible to adjust their visual mechanics as well. That's the contention of Tony Abbatine, director of national instruction for the Frozen Rope's Training Centers and the chain's medical advisor on vision. Since 1992, Frozen Ropes' researchers have studied the differences between the visual functions of pro baseball players and the general population, testing some 1,500 major- and minor-league players.

Among other conclusions in Frozen Ropes' white paper on the subject is that pro players have better visual acuity and depth perception than other people. They also have better contrast sensitivity, the ability to track a white ball against the stands or against a cloudy sky. There's more to it, though, than natural ability, according to the researchers. "Although visual acuity, stereo acuity, and contrast sensitivity are important to baseball excellence, they alone are not enough to make a major league player," the researchers concluded. "In order for a player to be successful, he must learn to integrate and master these visual functions while playing in a game."

That means visual memory is important—"an object's representation is stored and its memory recalled for future similar tasks. A superior player must use visual functions to quickly and properly identify the fine details of an object (such as a pitch or a fly ball), in order to produce a mental image of the object and allow for correct identification the next time an identical or similar object is seen. This may be important in recognizing the spin of the ball as it leaves the pitcher's hand or the movement of the pitch as it moves along its initial trajectory."

To that end, Frozen Ropes has developed a vision-training computer program called "Scope and Rope" that's used by professional baseball players as well as the youngsters among its clients. It is composed of two different visual exercises to challenge pitch recognition and visual motility, both of which the company contends are trainable.

TRAINING NOTES

by FRANK VIZARD

BRAIN OVER PAIN

Pain is all in your head. You might argue against this point the next time you finish a workout and your muscles feel sore. But according to neuroscientists who study the brain, the pain is actually in your head—more specifically, in an area of the cortex called the somatosensory strip. Each part of the body is represented on the strip, and each section on the strip is sized according to its relative sensitivity. Electrical signals from the muscle nerves activate the appropriate section of the strip as a warning signal that the body is overexerting itself. Endomorphins released by the brain block the incoming signals and allow the body to continue to function.

This relationship between the mind and athletic performance is coming under increasing scrutiny by scientists and has been explored in films like IMAX's *Wired to Win: Surviving the Tour de France.* Dr. Martin A. Samuels, a professor of neurology at Harvard Medical School who served as a science advisor on the film, believes that the mind can be used to regulate pain. "You don't need pills to reduce pain," Samuels says. "You can do it inside your head."

Samuels cites the ability of athletes to focus on the activity at hand and put pain in the background. This ability seems to come with training, Samuels says, as initial pain warnings are subsumed with experience gained by repetitive motion. "Muscle memory," as it is sometimes called, is located in the cerebellum rather than in individual muscles. "While clearly there is a genetic capacity that gives us a ceiling we can't go beyond," Samuels says, "hard work and training trumps genetics for most of us. The key to success is in your brain."

So it turns out lactic acid got a bum rap. For years, lactic acid was condemned as being your worst enemy. Now it turns out to be your best friend.

Anyone who's ever exercised knows what lactic acid is. It's what makes your muscles burn and cramp up. The theory went something like this: Lack of oxygen to the muscles leads to a buildup of lactic acid that leads to muscle fatigue.

Wrong. According to groundbreaking research done in 2006 by Dr. George A. Brooks, a biology professor at the University of California, Berkeley, lactic acid is not a debilitating waste product but a source of fuel. Muscles produce lactic acid from glucose, and they burn it for energy. The lactic acid is used as fuel by mitochondria, the energy-producing power plants inside cells.

So why are you experiencing pain? It's because your muscles haven't learned to burn lactic acid very well. Training helps your muscles convert the lactic acid into fuel more efficiently. In time, the pain goes away as your body adapts. That soreness you experience days later isn't from lactic acid, which dissipates within an hour after you stop exercising. More likely, it's due to minor muscle tears.

Still, despite the mix-up, coaches managed to instruct athletes to do the right thing even if it was for the wrong reasons. Coaches

Tyson Gay falls during the first quarterfinal heat of the men's 200 meter race at the U.S. Olympic Track and Field trials in 2008.

knew that performances improved when athletes worked on their endurance. As it turns out, endurance training increases the mitochondrial mass, allowing muscles to burn lactic acid better and longer.

As for the scientists, they now know what coaches suspected.

SOLDIERS LOVE KETTLEBELLS

In an age of fancy, high-tech gym equipment, some of the toughest  guys in the world are embracing old-fashioned kettlebells as their workout gear of choice. Frontline soldiers, including elite U.S. Navy SEAL teams, are using kettlebells to stay in shape. Developed centuries ago in Russia, kettlebells look like cannonballs with handles, and they come in a range of weights from nine to 106 pounds. And while their portability may make them attractive to soldiers on the move, that's not the reason they're popular. Kettlebells are at the heart of a training regimen based on repetition that makes you strong but bulk-free. Big muscles, it turns out, are less useful in combat where quick movement, speed, agility, and flexibility more often come into play, particularly in rugged, hostile terrain. As one kettlebell-swinging soldier put it, combat is about moving explosively for four to ten feet with what amounts to a small child on your back. What's more, no one on the battlefield asks to see the size of your biceps—strong cores are much more useful for carrying packs and ammo—and you rarely have to bench-press anything. Quick workouts with kettlebells are keeping soldiers at peak strength. The most avid fans of kettlebells enter competitions called Girevoy Sport, after the Russian word for kettleball—*girya*.

TEMPERATURE PILL IS A LIFESAVER

It sounds like something out of a science-fiction film, but for athletes prone to potentially life-threatening attacks of heatstroke and dehydration, their first line of defense may be an ingestible temperature pill that monitors internal core body temperature and  alerts athletic trainers in the event of trouble.

The CorTemp pill, made by HQ Inc. of Palmetto, Florida, is about the size of a multivitamin. An athlete takes the pill a few hours before engaging in an activity, so the pill has time to settle into the lower intestine, where the most stable internal core body temperature readings can be measured. Inside the pill is a temperature-sensitive quartz crystal oscillator, whose vibrations transmit frequencies that are relative to core temperature within the body. Powered by a tiny battery, electronic components transmit the pill's frequencies harmlessly through the body to a handheld data recorder that converts the signal to digital temperature format. The pill stays in the body on average between 24 and 36 hours before being eliminated.

The CorTemp pill is registered with the U.S. Food and Drug Administration (FDA) and works on a low-powered frequency suitable for use in humans. Readings from the pill are easily taken on the sidelines by athletic trainers who hold a data recorder close to the small of an athlete's back. The pill's signal can be transmitted long range up to a 300-foot line-of-sight distance, and multiple athletes can be monitored on a personal digital assistant (PDA) from the sidelines.

The CorTemp pill, which has already been widely adopted in football, where intense summer workouts are common, has been credited with heat-stress interventions even among players who exhibited no symptoms. Pro football and collegiate teams are especially sensitive to this issue after Minnesota Vikings offensive lineman Korey Stringer and University of Florida fullback Eraste Autin died of heatstroke in 2001 during a preseason practice.

The CorTemp ingestible temperature pill is based on technology developed for the National Aeronautics and Space Administration (NASA) to monitor astronauts aboard space shuttles. John Glenn, for example, used one for his return to space at the age of 77 in 1998.

CAN TOO MUCH WATER KILL YOU?

Drink plenty of water to avoid dehydration. That's what athletes have been told for years. But under certain circumstances, that very advice can kill you. The problem is called hyponatremia, a condition that occurs when blood-sodium levels drop dangerously low during intense exercise. If left untreated, hyponatremia can be fatal.

The athletes most susceptible to hyponatremia are those in endurance activities and who are tempted to consume excessive amounts of water or sports drink. Marathon runners clocking slow times of over four hours, for example, are often cited as being vulnerable as they may add four to eight pounds by the end of the race, all of it from fluids. Elite marathon runners may spend less than 30 seconds drinking over a two-hour period. Because the kidneys cannot excrete excess water during intense exercise, the extra water moves into their cells. This process becomes particularly dangerous when the water moves into brain cells,

which have no room to expand. These engorged brain cells press against the skull and compress the brain stem, which controls breathing, with possibly fatal results.

These findings, first reported by the *New England Journal of Medicine*, make the issue of hydration more complex than ever. At the other end of the scale, dehydration can lead to heat exhaustion and heatstroke; the latter is responsible for the deaths of a number of gear-laden football players practicing in late-summer workouts in recent years. Many of those fatalities were among high-school players, and doctors note that the young often do a poor job of keeping themselves hydrated. The American Council on Exercise suggests drinking 8 ounces of water a half hour prior to a 60-minute workout, 4 to 8 ounces every 10 to 15 minutes during exercise, and another 8 ounces within 30 minutes of finishing. This last bit of water intake may be the most important to remember, as studies have shown that players often don't replenish the fluids they've lost before the next practice session begins, thereby increasing their susceptibility to heat injury. Symptoms of heat stress can include pale color, bright red flushing, dizziness, headache, fainting, vomiting, and feeling hot or cold. Changes in performance or personality also are warning signs.

As for marathoners, sip while you run, advise doctors. If you stop to drink a couple of cups, you're drinking too much.

WILL GENE DOPING CREATE A SUPER-ATHLETE?

by FRANK VIZARD

IT STARTED WITH THE IDEA OF DEVELOPING A GENETIC TEST FOR ATHLETES WHO MAY BE SUSCEPTIBLE TO HYPERTROPHIC CARDIOMYOPATHY (HCM), A POTENTIALLY DEADLY HARDENING OF THE WALLS OF THE HEART THAT IS RESPONSIBLE FOR AS MANY AS ONE-THIRD OF SUDDEN-DEATH CASES AMONG ATHLETES UNDER 35. THEN CAME THE LAW OF UNINTENDED CONSEQUENCES COMMONLY REFERRED TO AS "BLOWBACK." THE LEAP FROM A DNA TEST FOR HCM TO A GENETIC TEST THAT MIGHT INDICATE ATHLETIC POTENTIAL IN A SPECIFIED SPORT WAS A SHORT ONE.

Genetic Technologies Corporation, based in Australia, now offers, for a small fee, a genetic test for the ACTN3 gene that encodes a protein found in fast-twitching muscle fibers crucial to sprinters and other power athletes. Conversely, the presence of two copies of an ACTN3 mutation called R577X means the protein is not produced, perhaps indicating that endurance-oriented sports may be a better calling for the athlete being tested. Other researchers link a gene associated with angiotensin converting enzyme (ACE) to endurance abilities.

Whether testing for the presence of a particular gene proves effective remains to be seen. But in the short term, the presence or lack of ACTN3 and any other sports-related genes that will be discovered will certainly be among the data that coaches use in training athletes, particularly those at elite levels where even the smallest edge can be the difference between winning and losing.

GENETIC MANIPULATION

The real test may come when DNA testing is harnessed to gene therapy to produce athletes whose abilities are enhanced to their highest degree. The World Anti-Doping Agency (WADA) has already placed such gene doping on its list of prohibited substances and methods, even before any evidence of its existence. With gene manipulation already being done in animals, the worry is that a genetically enhanced super-athlete who is able to run faster, jump higher, and throw farther is not far behind. WADA views gene doping as an inevitability to be practiced by unscrupulous labs of the BALCO (Bay Area Laboratory Cooperative) variety that rocked Major League Baseball by supplying illegal steroids to players.

Most misused drugs in sports are originally created to treat diseases and are considered groundbreaking when developed. Gene therapy represents a giant step forward in the treatment of illnesses, but gene doping could also threaten the integrity of all sports.

Gene doping is simple in theory and not beyond the ability of many of the well-trained people in labs all over the world, noted Dr. Theodore Freidmann, chairman of a WADA panel on gene doping, in a 2005 interview. The technology is evolving very rapidly. Scientists have already experimented with genes that produce insulin-growth factor (IGF-1) to help muscles grow and repair themselves. In these experiments genes are injected using a harmless virus as a carrier. The virus penetrates the cell and delivers its genetic payload. The added genes allow the body to produce more IGF-1 than it would normally, thereby speeding the healing of damaged muscles or strengthening weakened knees and other joints.

For athletes already injecting EPO (Erythropoietin) to enhance performance, gene doping would be the next logical step. Instead of injecting EPO, they would inject themselves with the gene that would allow the body to naturally produce more oxygen-carrying red blood cells to increase muscle endurance.

THE RISKS OF GENE DOPING

Gene doping is not without difficulties and risks. Newly inserted genes have to be able to produce the right amount of extra product at the right time to be effective. For example, after undergoing gene therapy, some French boys suffering from an extreme immune deficiency developed leukemia because the

Canadian sprinter Ben Johnson, a two-time Bronze Medal winner in the 1984 Olympics, won the Gold Medal for the 100-meter dash in the 1988 Olympics. After the win, he tested positive for steroids, and his Gold Medal and Olympic title were rescinded.

delivery system used to target the human cells was about as precise as a shotgun and adversely affected nontargeted cells. And unlike drugs that can be washed out of the body, gene doping can permanently alter the body's cellular structure and may have consequences that don't become evident for years.

TESTING FOR GENE DOPING

From WADA's perspective, the question now is whether gene doping can be detected. The organization already has a half-dozen research projects under way that use a variety of methodologies. One approach is to measure the effect of gene doping on red blood cells just as is done in drug testing. Another approach is to examine the effect of newly added genes on other nearby genes in the hope that an overall pattern or signature can be detected when gene doping occurs. Researchers also think full body scans like those used in magnetic resonance imaging can be developed to search for unusual genetic manifestations.

Whether gene doping can alter the competitive balance in sports remains to be seen, but if the history surrounding drug doping is any indicator, some unscrupulous athlete or lab is soon likely to embrace the possibility of a competitive advantage offered by gene doping.

DRUGS AND THEIR ABUSES

AMPHETAMINES: Commonly used as a stimulant in the treatment of attention-deficit disorder, Parkinson's disease, and narcolepsy. Some athletes take them to build muscle mass, increase endurance, recover more quickly from injury, and stay awake. Long-term abuse includes a weakened immune system, heart problems, and liver, kidney, and lung damage.

ANDROSTENEDIONE: "Andro" is an anabolic steroid that boosts the production of testosterone to build body mass and improve strength and endurance. Side effects in women are development of male characteristics (deepened voice and male-pattern baldness); in men, diminished sperm production, shrinkage of testicles, and enlargement of breasts; for both genders, an increased risk of heart attack or stroke from a lowering of "good" HDL cholesterol.

DARBEPOETIN: Used to treat kidney failure and cancer patients in chemotherapy. This peptide hormone boosts production of red blood cells that carry oxygen to the muscles, thereby increasing endurance levels. The most frequently reported serious adverse reactions are thrombosis, heart failure, sepsis, and cardiac arrhythmia.

>>>

DEHYDROEPIANDROSTERONE: DHEA is an anabolic agent used to treat a wide variety of illnesses ranging from cardiovascular disease to obesity. Some athletes use it to reduce body fat and promote muscle growth. Side effects may include stunted growth in teens, palpitations, extensive growth of body hair, hair loss, and liver damage.

DIURETICS: Used in weight-reduction programs. Athletes take these masking agents to flush steroids from their systems because the drug increases urine production. Side effects may include palpitations, muscle cramps and weakness, incontinence, kidney damage, and impaired hearing.

EPHEDRINE: Found in cold and allergy medicines, ephedrine is a stimulant that makes the heart beat faster, used to reduce fatigue and boost performance during short bursts of effort. Adverse reactions include dizziness, gastrointestinal distress, chest pain, seizures, and heatstroke.

ERYTHROPOIETIN: EPO is a peptide hormone used to boost the red blood cell count of cancer and AIDS patients. In an athlete, this synthetic version of a naturally occurring hormone increases aerobic capacity and muscle endurance. It also causes circulatory strain as well as clotting in smaller blood vessels.

HUMAN GROWTH HORMONE: This peptide hormone is used to help stunted children grow normally. Athletes can use it to build muscles, reduce body fat, and aid in recovery from strenuous workouts. Side effects may include arthritis-like symptoms, diabetes, abnormal growth of bones and internal organs, hardening of the arteries, and high blood pressure.

INSULIN: Diabetics use insulin to control blood-sugar levels, but athletes can use it in conjunction with steroids to build muscle and increase endurance and stamina. Possible side effects include weight gain, hypoglycemia, and sudden drops in blood sugar that can lead to a potentially fatal coma.

METHAMPHETAMINE: Used to treat obesity and attention-deficit disorder, "speed" can increase an athlete's level of alertness. Side effects can include high blood pressure, damage to blood vessels in the brain, hyperthermia, hypertension, and cardiovascular collapse.

MODAFINIL: Used to treat narcolepsy, it can also be used to increase alertness. Side effects may include depression, loss of muscle strength, lung problems, amnesia, and asthma.

NANDROLONE: An anabolic agent used to treat wasting diseases and build muscle mass in HIV-infected patients, it can also be used to increase muscle mass and strength in athletes. It occurs naturally but only in tiny quantities. Side effects may include liver damage, sterility, baldness, breast enlargement in men, and male characteristics in women.

NORANDROSTERONE: Found in nutritional supplements, it can be used to build muscle mass and increase strength. Side effects may include liver damage, sterility, baldness, breast enlargement in men, and male characteristics in women.

STANOZOLOL: Used to treat an episodic swelling condition called hereditary angioedema, it can also be used to increase strength and recover more quickly from workouts. Side effects may include liver damage, sterility, baldness, breast enlargement in men, and male characteristics in women.

TESTOSTERONE: Used in the treatment of conditions ranging from impotence to HIV, synthetic versions of the male sex hormone increase strength and muscle mass in athletes. Side effects may include liver damage, sterility, high blood pressure, shrinkage of testicles, enlarged prostate, breast enlargement in men, and male characteristics in women.

TETRAHYDROGESTRINONE: Nicknamed "The Clear," THG is a synthetic anabolic steroid that helps build body mass and improves strength and endurance; side effects are the same as synthetic testosterone. Unlike other anabolic steroids, which are pharmaceuticals intended for veterinary or human use, THG has never been approved for any medical indication.

TOP ELEVEN DOPING SCANDALS

[1] **TOUR DE FRANCE:** The world's most famous bicycle race has been tarnished by the seemingly never-ending association of riders with performance-enhancing drugs in 1998, 2002, 2004, 2006, and 2007. In 2012, Lance Armstrong, who had won seven consecutive times from 1999 to 2005, was stripped of those victories and banned for life from competition after a report

>>>

Lance Armstrong came forward to confess after allegations of widespread doping in the Tour de France became public in 2012.

disclosed that he used performance-enhancing drugs. Armstrong had always vehemently denied the allegations of his doping, but once the facts came out, he came forward to confess that he had started taking performance-enhancing drugs in the mid-1990s and that his "cocktail" of choice was banned testosterone, EPO, and transfusions using his own tainted blood.

[2] **EAST GERMANY:** An Olympic powerhouse in the 1970s and 1980s, the former Communist nation doubled its Gold Medal count from 20 to 40 in just four years. After the fall of the Berlin Wall, it was revealed that athletes often were unknowingly doped starting as young as thirteen.

[3] **1983 PAN-AMERICAN GAMES:** A surprise test for steroid use nailed American triple Gold Medal winner Jeff Michaels as well as other weightlifters. Michaels was stripped of his medals. Dozens of other athletes withdrew

from the competition, heralding the modern age of drug testing.

[4] **THE BALCO AFFAIR:** In 2003, an anonymous track-and-field coach leaked the names of athletes using the steroid THG and provided a used syringe to the U. S. Anti-Doping Administration (USADA). The leak led to the BALCO affair, the conspiracy to provide previously undetectable steroids to athletes in many sports, most notably in baseball and track-and-field events. Top athletes fell under suspicion, and some were suspended from their sports when urine samples were found to have traces of THG.

[5] **BEN JOHNSON:** The Canadian sprinter narrowly edged out Carl Lewis in the 100-meter dash for the Gold Medal in the 1988 Seoul Olympics but then tested positive for steroids, heightening concern about the use of drugs in sports. Johnson was disqualified.

[6] **MAJOR LEAGUE BASEBALL, 1998:** Mark McGwire admitted to the then-legal use of andro after breaking the single-season home run record in 2001, while Barry Bonds broke McGwire's record and passed Hank Aaron on the all-time list under a cloud of suspicion that now pervaded the sport. In December of 2007, the Mitchell Report named 89 players that had ties to performance enhancing drugs and hormones. Senator George Mitchell was appointed by MLB commissioner Bud Selig in March of 2006 to investigate the use of performance enhancing drugs in professional baseball. Among the players named in the report that allegedly used or had ties to PED use were superstars Barry Bonds and Roger Clemens. The report led to a stricter drug policy that enforces a 50 game suspension for a first time violation, 100 game suspension for a second violation and a lifetime ban for a third violation. Notable players that have been suspended have been Rafael Palmeiro and Manny Ramirez. In 2012, All-Star Game MVP

Melky Cabrera, who was leading all of baseball with a .346 batting.

[7] **CHINA'S SWIMMERS:** Between 1990 and 2000, 40 Chinese swimmers failed drug tests, triple the number of any other country.

[8] **THE WHISKEY TEST:** Irish swimmer Michelle Smith came out of nowhere to win three Gold Medals and one Silver Medal in the 1996 Atlanta Olympics while also managing to evade drug testers. Caught at home in a surprise test, Smith used alcohol to tamper with her urine sample and got a four-year suspension.

[9] **CROSS-COUNTRY SKIING:** EPO and steroids joined ski wax in the kits of competitors in the 2001 World Nordic Championships and at the 2002 Salt Lake Olympics, where several athletes tested positive for banned substances and were stripped of their medals.

[10] **NANDROLONE:** By 2005, it achieved status as the most widely used steroid in athletics, but occassionally its use may be inadvertent as it is found in improperly labeled diet supplements, energy drinks, and vitamins.

[11] **MAJOR LEAGUE BASEBALL, 2013:** In 2013, two former league MVPs, Alex Rodriguez and Ryan Braun, were among 14 major and minor league players suspended by Major League Baseball for obtaining performance-enchancing drugs from an anti-aging clinic in Florida. Rodriguez was banned for 211 games and Braun 65, while the remaining 12 players got 50 game suspensions. All but Rodriguez, who appealed, accepted their suspensions.

Baseball

THE MACHINE THAT SHATTERS BASEBALL MYTHS

by STEVE ROUSSEAU

This article appeared in
POPULAR MECHANICS in 2011.

WITH A HANDFUL OF BASEBALLS, A FEW BATS AND AN AIR CANNON, A NUCLEAR PHYSICIST AND A MECHANICAL ENGINEER SET OUT TO BUST SOME OF BASEBALL'S MOST PROLIFIC HITTING MYTHS: CORKED BATS, JUICED BALLS AND HUMIDORS. MEET THE MACHINE BUILT TO TEST THESE AGE-OLD ARGUMENTS.

Derek Jeter of the New York Yankees is a lifetime .300 hitter.

Some baseball fans are content simply to watch the game they love. And then there are fans who happen to be scientists.

Physicist Alan Nathan of the University of Illinois and mechanical engineer Lloyd Smith of Washington State University wanted to put some of the biggest baseball myths out there—corked bats, juiced balls, and the effect of humidity—to the test. Because collecting measurements on a live batter is next to impossible, Nathan says, the team turned to an advanced testing lab that Smith designed at Washington State.

HOW IT'S MADE

Developed in 2002, Smith's testing system measures the burst of a ball off the bat with three key instruments. There's a 12-foot air cannon delivery system including a sabot—a plastic carriage that guides the ball down the tube—a box of three light screens to measure ball speed and a bat pivot to hold the bat in place.

First, the scientists place a baseball onto a polycarbonate sabot and load it into the cannon. Since the bat is stationary and there's no batter swinging it, Smith's setup must accelerate the baseball to a speed that combines both the velocity of a major league pitch and the bat speed of a major league hitter: about 150 miles per hour. The sabot fits precisely within the cannon's tube, and even at that crazy speed it can keep a baseball along a straight path with little spin or deviation. The stability the sabot provides is the key to hitting the sweet spot and accurately testing the pop in a bat.

The air cannon blast ejects both the sabot and the baseball from its barrel, so Smith designed an arrestor plate to stop the sabot and allow the ball to fly free. "That arrestor plate is, in my opinion, kind of a cool design," Smith says. To soften the blow of the sabot, the plate rides on four pneumatic shocks. Yet even this wasn't enough, so he designed the arrestor plate to be moving backward when it catches the sabot, cradling it to soften the impact. "It's kind of as if you were trying to catch a baseball without a mitt."

The baseball then flies free into the light box, which contains three light screens designed to measure the ball's speed. As the ball passes through each screen, the time is recorded. With these three separate times, Nathan and Smith can calculate the speed of the ball both as it enters the box and after it hits the bat and rebounds backward.

Those speed measurements allow the researchers to calculate what they call the coefficient of restitution (COR). "[It's] the bounciness of the ball off the bat," Nathan says, and it's the primary metric the team uses for testing bats—and busting baseball myths. In a ball–bat collision, the energy is shared between both the ball and the bat. That gives a wooden bat a COR of just under 0.5. Hollow aluminum bats tend to have a higher COR, though, because of the "trampoline effect," Nathan explains. "Instead of going to compress the baseball, which is what happens when it's hitting a rigid surface, it goes into compressing the wall of the bat, and that energy is very effectively returned back to the ball again."

Smith's system is so effective that the NCAA uses it to regulate its bat performance standards. But for a new study, he and Nathan set to testing three of the most debated myths in baseball.

CORKED BATS

Corked bats are one of the most notorious examples of baseball cheating, but the researchers suggest it might not do much good: When testing corked bats, Nathan and his team found that instead of increasing trampoline effect, corking a wooden bat actually reduced it. "What you gain in higher bat speed, you lose in a less effective collision," Nathan says. "It does not lead to a higher batted ball speed." And because the bat is lighter, balls hit with a corked bat don't travel as far, he says. However, the lighter weight of a corked bat may allow hitters to get to pitches they might not otherwise hit with a standard bat.

JUICED?

When baseballs were flying out of the park in the late 1990s and early 2000s, speculation abounded that the balls—and not just the players—were juiced. Nathan and Smith wanted to see if modern baseballs truly are livelier than those used decades ago. So they fired two sets of balls, one from the 2004 season and one from the late 1970s, against a steel plate, and measured the COR. The result? Identical COR figures between balls present and past, suggesting that the difference was in the players.

HUMIDORS

In the 1990s, Coors Field in Denver was a launching pad. The home of the Colorado Rockies set the major league record in 1999 with 303 home runs in a single season. This was presumably caused in part by the stadium's high elevation, which meant that batted balls encountered less air resistance. But the Rockies got tired of seeing their pitchers beaten up in slugfest after slugfest, and so the organization began to keep game baseballs in a humidor, hoping the added weight and size would make the balls come back to earth more quickly.

Nathan and Smith tested out the humidor-baseball idea in the lab, and, indeed, they found that a relative-humidity increase from 30 percent to 50 percent would result in a COR decrease of 0.024. That might not sound like much, but Nathan says it would cause an average reduction of 14 feet on fly balls, cutting home run probability by 25 percent. Home run statistics from Coors Field agree with Nathan and Smith's conclusions: They were down from 3.29 per game in the pre-humidor era (1995–2001) to 2.39 per game in the humidor era (2002–2010).

SPLIT-FINGER SORCERY?

Now that he's tested some of the game's most common hitting myths, Nathan wants to turn his attention to pitching. While he was watching a game recently, one split-finger fastball by Yankee pitcher Freddy Garcia caught his eye. "The ball breaks in a direction that doesn't agree with our common perception of how it should break, given how it's spinning."

Though the game has been played professionally for more than a century, there still are plenty of curiosities to be put to the test in the lab. "The players, they know how the game is played," he says. "I'm just trying to understand, or put in some firm physics basis what they already intuitively understand."

HOW BASEBALL HAS CHANGED SINCE THE 1920S

by DAVIN COBURN

Here are four ways baseball has evolved since the 1920s:

[1] **BIGGER GUNS:** Weight training and performance-enhancing drugs have helped out at the plate. According to baseball-reference.com, there were 1.12 homers per game in the 2001 season—three times more than in 1927.

[2] **BETTER BALLS:** You can't hit what you can't see. Until 1920, baseballs were often covered in tobacco juice. After Cleveland Indians shortstop Ray Chapman was killed by a pitch thrown by New York Yankees hurler Carl Mays in the spitball was replaced by clean, white balls.

[3] **SLICKER PITCHES:** Cut fastballs, split-fingers, and sliders keep hitters off their heels. The year 2001 saw 6.67 strikeouts per game—almost 2.5 times more than in 1927.

[4] **SMALLER ZONES:** With a 17-inch-wide plate, a 6-foot-2-inch player in 1927, like Babe Ruth, had a strike zone of roughly 545 square inches. By 2001, rule changes shrank the zone of a 6-foot-2-inch player, like Barry Bonds, to about 410 square inches.

ANATOMY OF
A SWING

by DAVIN COBURN

IN LESS TIME THAN IT TAKES TO BLINK, PRO HITTERS ROUTINELY ACHIEVE THE EXTRAORDINARY.

When Ryan Zimmerman stands at the plate, there's no time to analyze physics. "I'm thinking about what the pitcher might throw in that situation," says the Washington Nationals third baseman. "I have to eliminate as many options as I can before he releases the ball." Zimmerman has hit at least 20 home runs in a season five times. Let's stop the clock to examine ball spin, bat speed, and the rest of what Zimmerman instinctively understands about hitting. Here's how those home runs happened.

SPIN CONTROL

A fastball comes to the plate with backspin—up to 1,800 revolutions per minute (rpm). To hit the ball out of the park, a batter must reverse the rotation of the ball so that it leaves the bat with backspin. This gives the ball lift.

A curveball can carry topspin of 1,900 rpm, making it bite downward as it crosses the plate. By crushing a curve, a batter builds on the pitcher's topspin—producing 45 percent more backspin off the bat.

The result? Curveballs can be hit farther. Mont Hubbard of the University of California, Davis, found that a 94-mile-per-hour (mph) fastball leaves the bat 3 mph faster than a 78-mph curveball—but it travels 442 feet compared to the curve's 455 feet.

BAT SPEED VERSUS MASS

Boosting two factors—the mass of the bat and the speed of the swing—can raise batted ball speed (BBS), which adds distance to a hit. But swing speed can affect BBS more dramatically.

Research has shown that doubling the weight of a 20-ounce wood bat can raise BBS of 68.5 mph to 80.4 mph—a 17.3 percent increase. But Daniel Russell, a professor at Kettering University in Michigan, found that doubling the swing speed of a 30-ounce bat can raise a BBS of 62 mph to 83.8 mph—a 35.1 percent increase.

In terms of turning a hit into a homer: against a 94-mph fastball, every 1-mph increase in swing speed extends distance about 8 feet.

Ryan Zimmerman, third baseman for the Washington Nationals, at bat against the Colorado Rockies at RFK Stadium, in Washington, D.C., in June 2006.

THE IDEAL BAT

University of Arizona professor Terry Bahill found that the maximum bat weight before swing speed drops is about 41 ounces. But a pro player's ideal bat weight, he says, is lighter—in the 31- to 32-ounce range. This weight produces a BBS 1 percent below the BBS of the maximum-weight bat—allowing the batter greater maneuverability with a negligible loss of power.

Zimmerman has discovered the same principle with his 34-inch, 32-ounce MaxBat. "A bigger bat obviously has more solid wood," he says, "but you can handle a smaller bat better."

FORCING THE ISSUE

Major-league baseballs have an average mass of 5.125 ounces, and a 90-mph fastball can leave the bat at 110 mph. Extrapolating Newton's second law of motion, Russell determined that, in a collision lasting less than one-thousandth of a second, the average pro swing imparts 4,145 pounds of force to the ball. Peak forces exceed 8,300 pounds—enough to stop a Mini Cooper, rolling at 10 mph, in its tracks.

MAXING OUT

Contrary to the lore surrounding historic, titanic blasts—like Mickey Mantle's fabled 565-foot shot in 1953—physicists estimate that the farthest a man can hit a ball, at sea level, without help from the wind, is about 475 feet.

A SUPERSIZE SWEET SPOT

A bat vibrates at multiple frequencies when it collides with a ball. How much energy is transferred to the ball—instead of spread through the bat and the batter's hands—depends on where the collision occurs. A bat vibrating at its fundamental frequency (below, in black) has a node of zero vibration about $6\frac{1}{2}$ inches from the barrel end (Node 1). This was long thought to be the bat's sweet spot. But Rod Cross, a physicist at Australia's University of Sydney, found that the spot is more like a zone. At a second frequency (in red), a bat has another node about $4\frac{1}{2}$ inches down the barrel (Node 2). Hits between the two produce minimal vibration—and transfer more energy—at both frequencies. "Every ball I've hit that I haven't felt, I knew I hit well," Zimmerman says.

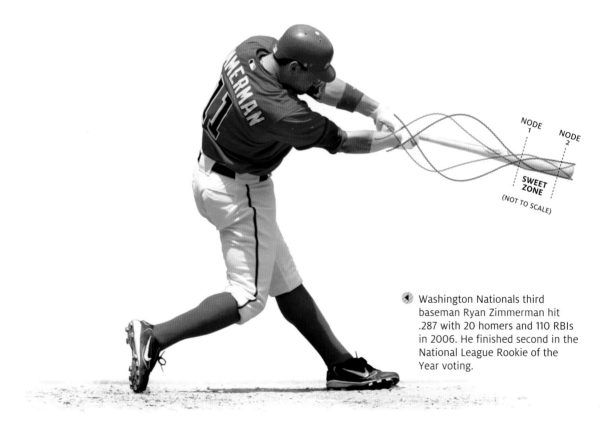

Washington Nationals third baseman Ryan Zimmerman hit .287 with 20 homers and 110 RBIs in 2006. He finished second in the National League Rookie of the Year voting.

THINKING QUICKLY

A 90-mph fastball can reach home plate in 400 milliseconds—or four-tenths of a second. But a batter has just a quarter-second to identify the pitch, decide whether to swing, and start the process. "Once the pitch is in flight, it's the snap of your fingers," Zimmerman says. What happens next is "pretty much just instinct." A batter takes 100 milliseconds to see the three-inch ball, and 75 milliseconds to identify spin, speed, and pitch location. The batter has another 50 milliseconds to decide whether to swing, and where, before he must act. It can take nearly 25 milliseconds for the brain's signals to pulse through the hitter's body and start his legs moving. The swing itself takes 150 milliseconds.

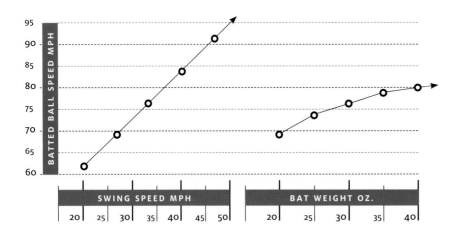

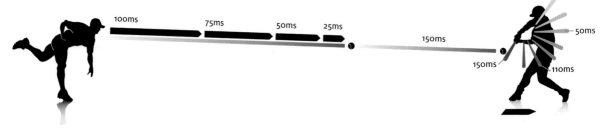

For the first 50 milliseconds of a swing, a batter can stop his two-pound bat in time to check the swing. By 110 milliseconds, the bat, moving at up to 80 mph, carries too much inertia to be stopped.

HOW TO HIT A HOMER

by LOU PINIELLA

This article appeared in
POPULAR MECHANICS in 1991.

THE HOME RUN CAN WIN A BALL GAME FOR YOU WITH ONE SWING OF THE BAT. NO QUESTION. IT'S THE MOST EXCITING HIT IN BASEBALL. BY EXTENSION, THE GUYS WHO CAN SMASH A BASEBALL 400 FEET OR MORE OVER A FENCE ARE AMONG THE MOST EXCITING PLAYERS IN THE GAME.

How far can a baseball be hit? The old-timers talk about Mickey Mantle hitting one 565 feet. I've seen some audacious shots but never one in the 500-foot category. I'd say 450 to 475 feet is about as far as a human being can hit a baseball without help from the elements.

HITTING THEORIES

There are basically two schools of thought when it comes to hitting a baseball. One was developed by Ted Williams, the legendary Boston Red Sox slugger. The Williams school emphasizes a rotation of the hips to generate power.

The second school of thought is best articulated by Charley Lau, a former coach with the Kansas City Royals and New York Yankees, among others. The Lau school puts a premium on making contact with the ball. Lau asks you to keep your head down and shift your weight from back to front as you swing.

While Ted Williams was my idol as a child, I'm philosophically more in the Charley Lau school. If you throw your hips as Williams recommends, your hands are going to drag, and your swing is going to be a little longer. Your navel is going to lead, and your hands are going to catch up a little late.

With the Williams approach, it is much easier to hit the low ball. On the low pitch, you have more time to catch up to the ball. The higher a pitch is in the strike zone, the harder it is to catch up to it. Your swing has to be shorter and more compact.

The problem is that as the ball moves up the strike zone, it will hop a little more and have two to three miles per hour more velocity.

The hitting method I'm going to describe is fundamentally derived from the Lau school, but with a variation designed to deliver more power. Does it work? When Chris Sabo of the Cincinnati Reds used this approach, he upped his home run production from 6 to 25 homers in a year.

STANCE

What you want in your stance is balance. Balance allows you to do a lot of things. It allows you to get a good weight shift. It allows

Ryan Howard of the Philadelphia Phillies hit 58 home runs in 2006, his first full season in the major leagues.

you to go out after a breaking ball. It allows you to wait on an off-speed pitch.

The way George Brett of the Kansas City Royals stood in the batter's box was nice to see. The good hitter will lean forward across the plate and then shift his weight back. One way to set your balance in this manner is to reach across the plate with your bat. I used to do this every at bat. It was a great balancing trick for me. Brett did this also. He leaned out, touched the other side of the plate, and then he was ready to hit a baseball. He knew exactly how much extension he needed to the outside of the plate.

In terms of positioning the feet, the home run hitter cannot have a very closed stance—meaning one in which the front leg is closer to the plate than the back leg. Most of the guys hitting the ball out of the park have a slightly open or square stance. This means the front leg is a degree or two off a straight line that can

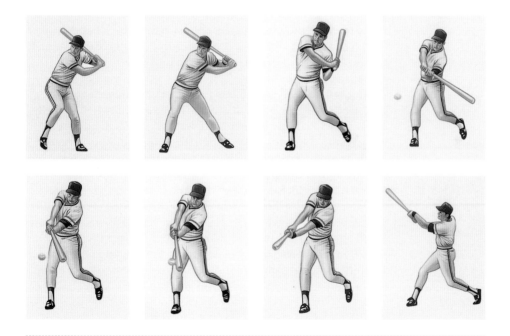

Home run hitters use a front-knee cock to get their weight back. The front knee acts like a trigger and also gets the batter's hands back. As the ball enters the hitting zone, the hands lead the body through the swing. The bottom hand provides the extension needed to cover the plate and supplies power. The top hand guides the bat. After contact is made, the hands grip the bat in the follow-through. This produces a total weight shift that helps generate the power needed to hit the ball out of the park.

be drawn from the back leg of the batter to the pitcher. Even if they start out slightly closed, they all wind up slightly open when they're done.

Home run hitters don't have very wide stances. Most stances are about a shoulder width—a position that allows them to stride and make good use of the weight transfer in their lower bodies when they swing.

Once you're in the batter's box, don't lock into a stance. There should be a little movement in the feet. Like a tennis player awaiting a serve, your feet should not be stationary. If a tennis player can return a fast-moving ball, that tells me you can get set to swing off movement more quickly than you can from a stationary position.

BODY MOVEMENT

All home run hitters have one thing in common—the front-knee cock. It's really their trigger to get everything going. When the knee cocks, you're shifting weight to the back leg and getting ready to drive off it. In baseball, you have to go back before you can go forward. As the knee is cocked, you can get a small turn at the hip and at the shoulder. This turning motion helps the hitter get his hands back.

At this point, the great home run hitters do something you can't teach. Amazingly, most of your home run hitters don't have a classic swing. Most of them have hitches—a little up-down motion with the bat at the start of their swing that's just innate. Hitch or no hitch, at this point there should be a straight line coming up from your back foot through your hip to the top of your back shoulder.

Your shoulders should be fairly horizontal at the start of the swing, but as you make contact, the front shoulder is going to be a little higher than your back shoulder. This is because there is no such thing as a level swing. Everyone swings slightly up. Home run hitters swing slightly more up than other hitters. The higher up you finish, the more power you get—not to mention lift.

BAT GRIP AND WEIGHT SHIFT

The bat should be held in a relaxed, loose grip. Somebody should be able to pull it out of your hands. The bottom hand should grip the bat a little more tightly than at the top. The bottom hand is the lead hand because this hand gives you the extension.

All home run hitters get bottom-hand extension. That's what gives them power. Everyone thinks the top hand gives you power, but the bottom hand provides most of it. The top hand steers the

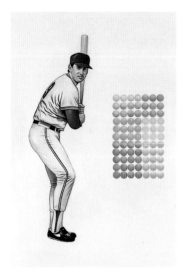

Some pitches are more likely to be hit out for home runs than others. Baseball people always tell pitchers to "keep it low." The truth is most home runs come on down-and-in fastballs and breaking balls that let hitters fully extend. More home runs are hit when the ball is in the red zone. The orange zone is number two and the yellow zone is number three. It becomes progressively more difficult to hit a home run when the ball is in the green, blue, and purple zones. The blue zone jumps to the number one spot for hanging breaking balls.

bat. If the top hand dominates the swing, the bat will be in and out of the hitting area very quickly. With bottom-hand extension, you stay in the hitting area much longer.

Now, here's where I disagree with Lau and his disciples. They suggest bottom-hand extension, but with top-hand release of the bat upon contact. I don't agree with that because you lose power. You're not getting the back side of your body to drive through the ball.

If you look at your home run hitter, there isn't one who lets the top hand go off the bat. The bottom hand gets the hitter to the ball. The top hand gets the hitter through the ball. By holding on to the bat with both hands into the follow-through, you get a total weight shift that delivers more power into the swing.

You let go of the bat only when you've driven all the way through the ball—when it's no longer physically possible to hold on to the bat because the bottom hand has extended well beyond the top hand's ability to hang on. At this point, your back foot is slightly off the ground or has pivoted so only the toe is touching the dirt.

With the Lau method, you get a pretty good lateral weight shift, but not a total weight shift. Without a total weight shift, you can't generate the power to drive the ball out of the park as consistently. With Lau, the front foot may skate forward a little and the top hand leaves the bat upon contact. There is no trigger or top-hand follow-through to generate a total weight shift for power hitting. Likewise, I disagree with the Williams method of throwing the hips at the ball. I believe in throwing the hands at the ball and letting the hips follow the hands.

Technique helps a lot, of course, but a lot of what constitutes a home run hitter occurs naturally. There's the hitch, for one thing. Home run hitters also go to the ball more quickly. They don't take a long time deciding on whether or not to swing.

For the most part, home run hitters use a bat that is two to three ounces heavier than most, with a thinly tapered handle and lots of barrel on the end. It takes a man to swing it. Home run hitters want a club to slug the ball. When they connect properly, the ball is as likely to go out of the park as it is anywhere else.

BABE RUTH'S HOME RUN SECRETS

by A. A. ALBELLI

The famed New York Yankees slugger Babe Ruth (1895–1948) hit 714 home runs during a career that ended in 1935. Ruth's record stood until Hank Aaron of the Atlanta Braves broke it in 1974. This article appeared in POPULAR MECHANICS in 1928.

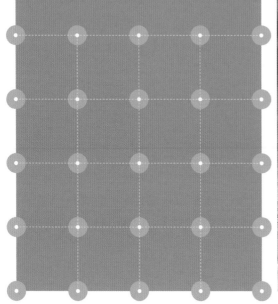

THAT STODGY URCHIN WHO USED TO CATCH FOR A SCHOOL BASEBALL TEAM YEARS AGO, NOW GROWN TO BE THE GREATEST FIGURE EVER KNOWN TO THE SPORT, TOLD ME THE OTHER DAY THAT HE EXPECTS TO CLOUT 100 HOME RUNS FOR THE NEW YORK YANKEES NEXT SEASON.

Babe Ruth at bat in New York: the Yankees vs. St. Louis Browns at the Polo Grounds on May 20, 1922. The following season, the Yankees moved into their new stadium—"The House That Ruth Built."

There is nothing of the braggadocio about Babe Ruth. He is all that baseball-loving America looks for in its idol. The halo which popularity has woven about him has not changed his boyish personality.

"The way I have come to feel," he said, "I can knock out 100 homers any old season from now on." During the 1927 season, he reached the record of 60 circuit drives. He added two more when the Yankees played the Pittsburgh Pirates in the World Series.

"The only thing that will prevent me from slamming out a century-fold of home runs," continued Babe Ruth, "will be unobliging pitchers. I mean, the boys on the mound are beginning to know what I pick at for good drives.

"They all know I hate a slow curve. It's no secret. What I like best of all is when they steam over fast ones. Those are the ones I like to nibble on every time.

"Then there's another thing. You know a lot of time a twirler will toss them at me and all around me, but never in line with a good swing. I am not accusing anyone of letting me walk to first intentionally. But you know, I kind of get that feeling."

"How would you explain, shall I say the mechanics, of your home run swatting?" I asked him.

The big fellow pondered a little while.

"Well, I'll tell you. It's hard to say which element comes first. Coordination, that is perfect timing and harmony of action, is a great essential. You have got to develop rhythm and full utility of every muscle. My whole body goes with every swing. I swing right from the hips. And those who have seen me take a healthy sock at the ball know what I mean. With that coordination there is the fact that I assume that strength is behind it."

During the season, Babe Ruth explained, he weighs around 210. He towers over six feet. His shoulders are broad and massive. Yet there is one incongruity. His wrists are very small.

"So, with this might and brawn which I try to keep in the pink of condition, I cannot help but feel that something is bound to happen to the ball when I lean on it. I might tell you I have another trick of keeping the right foot behind the left, not very

A close-up showing how the Babe gripped the the bat.

The highest-paid pair of batting eyes in the history of baseball carried the Babe to a new world's home run record last season, breaking his own previous mark. [Editor's note: This caption appeared in the original 1928 article.]

much. But that helps. I bat left-handed, you know.

"Then the eyes play a great part. Oh, yes, the eyes have got to be well-educated. I would be lost if I didn't have a sense of judgment which the eyes give me.

"As for trying to control the drive itself, I always aim to slam the ball out on a straight line. Pop flies are a little too dangerous. A lusty drive to the bleachers is sure to do the trick.

"There's a little buddy, we must not forget," said Ruth, picking up his bat. "Look it over."

It was very heavy, as bats go. It reminded me of the club of a Neanderthal man.

"It's the heaviest bat in baseball," he said. "It weighs 54 ounces.

"Now that we have the hitting of the ball done away with, there remains another very important job and that is circling the bases. I don't care what anyone says, but a batter is lost, no matter in what part of the field he hits the ball, if he cannot run fast.

"I came to appreciate that fact long ago. I don't do 100 yards in ten flat. But I'd bet I wouldn't come far from it. Being a speedy runner then is another very important factor.

"Of course, when the player is off the diamond, he must not think he can forget his condition. He has got to keep trim all the time. He has to follow a strict code. He must do nothing to impair his physical condition."

Babe Ruth, who has hit 416 home runs in the big leagues since he started with the Boston Red Sox in 1914, has had so glamorous a career that his name means as much to the American boy of today as the names of any three heroes from the pages of history.

"And I'm not through yet by any means, as you can judge what I said about 100 homers," he said. "I am now 33 and expect to be going strong at 44."

Ruth went on to tell the story of his life without any compunction, always clinging to a modest vein.

He was born in Baltimore, Maryland. His father was a factory hand. They were poor. At times his mother had to work in a mill

Knocking out a homer, a series showing Ruth as he steps to bat, facing the pitcher, starting the swing, in mid-swing, and finally, following through after the ball.

to help replenish the family larder.

George Herman Ruth, which is the home run king's real name, was healthy and husky as a boy. At the age of seven, he was sent to St. Mary's Industrial School in Baltimore. It was there that he got his first inkling of baseball. He started off by being the catcher of the team. In 1913, the school team already had a reputation. Babe Ruth was a southpaw pitcher about whom people were beginning to talk and predict things. He was also a good hitter.

That winter, Jack Dunn, then manager of the Baltimore Eastern-league outfit, saw Ruth. The lad was not yet twenty. Dunn wanted Ruth for his team but was told that he could not get him without legally adopting him, because he was still a minor, which he did.

The following season Ruth played with Dunn's team and then was sold to the Boston Americans for $10,000. His salary for that year, 1915, was to be $4,000. The Red Sox conceived the idea of relegating him to the outfield, so that he might conserve his strength when he came to bat.

THROWING HEAT

by JIM KAAT

This article appeared in POPULAR MECHANICS in 2004.

WITH A THREE-RUN LEAD GOING INTO THE BOTTOM OF THE EIGHTH INNING IN GAME 5 OF THE 2003 AMERICAN LEAGUE CHAMPIONSHIP SERIES, NO ONE WAS THE LEAST BIT SURPRISED WHEN NEW YORK YANKEES MANAGER JOE TORRE CALLED ON CLOSER MARIANO RIVERA TO COME IN AND SHUT DOWN THE BOSTON RED SOX.

New York Yankees ace reliever Mariano Rivera is arguably the best closer in the history of baseball.

Rivera, arguably the best closer in the history of baseball, got off to a shaky start, giving up a leadoff triple into the right-field corner by Todd Walker and an RBI groundout by Nomar Garciaparra. The next batter, fearsome slugger Manny Ramirez, had already homered in the game. Another score would bring Boston within one run of the Yankees. It was the classic confrontation—power against power. Ramirez versus Rivera.

But Manny Ramirez had a big advantage. Walking up to the plate, he already knew what Rivera was going to throw him. In fact, all 34,619 fans packed into Fenway Park that night knew what Rivera was going to throw. Essentially, Rivera throws only one pitch—a hard, heavy cut fastball that breaks slightly to the left just as it crosses the plate. Occasionally, he'll also throw a 98-mph four-seam fastball that comes straight across the plate, high in the strike zone. That's it.

Ramirez dug in and peered out at Rivera, gearing up for the fastball. Rivera came set and fired. The four-seamer, 98 miles per hour. Ramirez swung late and missed. Strike one. Rivera had thrown it right by him even though Ramirez knew it was coming. Rivera peered in at catcher Jorge Posada for the sign, came set, and fired. The cutter was low and away at 92 mph. Ramirez, way out in front this time, fouled it off. Strike two. You could see Ramirez scowl at Rivera, a determined look on his face. Ramirez would catch up with the next fastball. And it would be a fastball. He knew that. And he would catch up with it.

Rivera peered in, got the sign, came set, and delivered. A cutter, high and away. Ramirez, fooled, checked his swing and managed to lay off it. Ball one. You could almost hear Ramirez think. The next pitch was going to be a four-seamer. It had to be.

It was.

It was a perfect fastball, textbook perfect. It poured across the plate letter high, 98 mph. Ramirez, simply overmatched even though he had guessed right, swung late and limply. His feeble swing, barely completed as the ball thudded into Posada's mitt, was too little, too late. Rivera, who went on to take Most Valuable Player honors in the ALCS, had proved it again. The fastball is still the best pitch in baseball.

Four-Seamer

Two-Seamer

Dry Spitter

Split-Finger

Not only is the fastball a deadly weapon in its own right, it also is the basis for most pitchers' entire game strategies. Everything works off the fastball. Once you establish your fastball in a game, every batter has to be geared up for it since it might come on any given pitch. Once a pitcher has a batter in this over-tensed, hair-trigger state, it's much easier to fool him with off-speed and breaking pitches.

But it all starts with the fastball.

A fastball may have been the first pitch thrown in a baseball game, the pitcher attempting to simply overpower the batter. Since that first recorded game in 1846, there have been more variations of the fastball developed than any other pitch. Today, you'll find guys throwing a two-seam fastball, a four-seam fastball, a cut fastball, a split-finger fastball, and probably others. Here is a breakdown on how these pitches are thrown.

FOUR-SEAMER: The four-seam fastball is the king of the power pitches and can be delivered with the most accuracy. The grip side view shows how shallow the ball lies in the hand. The ball is held on the wide seams and is thrown over the top. As the ball is released, the fingertips impart straight backspin, with all four seams rotating. This produces a true pitch from the mound to the plate, so there is very little lateral movement.

TWO-SEAMER: The two-seam fastball is gripped with the fingers on the narrow seams. As with the four-seamer, you don't want the ball too deep in the hand; a deeper grip causes more pull and backspin. Fingertip pressure with either the middle or index finger against the seam generates sidespin, which causes the ball to drop as it nears the plate. This late movement is called a sinking or tailing fastball. Hurled by a lefty, the ball will move down and away from a right-handed hitter. Thrown by a right-handed pitcher, the ball will move down and away from a left-handed hitter. Whereas power pitchers favor the four-seam fastball, ground-ball pitchers use the two-seamer more.

THE CUTTER: The cut fastball, or cutter, is thrown using either of the above grips. The key is to keep your hand behind the ball as long as possible and let the grip pressure in the middle finger give it the sidespin or cut. The cutter will move in or out a few inches—like a tight slider—as it nears the plate, but it won't drop like the sinking fastball.

DRY SPITTER (pictured on the opposite page): The dry spitter is thrown with your fingers on the hide as opposed to the seams of the baseball. Before the spitter was made illegal, hurlers would put saliva on the ball to reduce friction, and it would sort of squirt out of their hand like a Ping-Pong ball. These days, the pitcher can have a little coating of mound dirt on his fingers. This also reduces friction. The ball comes out with virtually no spin and will sink as it reaches the plate.

SPLIT-FINGER (pictured on the opposite page): The split-finger fastball is released with relatively little spin. The ball has a tumbling rotation and a late downward movement—similar to the dry spitter. You can change the velocity of the split-finger pitch by varying the position and pressure of your fingers on the ball.

The fastball is the only pitch you can throw to all four quadrants of the strike zone, and it's not used nearly enough today. Look at a pitcher's best games, and I'll bet you'll see a high percentage of fastballs and good control. That's why (ex-Yankee) David Wells was so successful. He favors his fastball, and throws most of them for strikes. His stuff is consistent, from start to start, and he has very few arm problems. He trusts his fastball. To be successful, all pitchers, like Wells, need to trust their fastball and say, here it is, hit it if you can!

THE MYTH OF THE RISING FASTBALL

by PETER BRANCAZIO

Years ago, baseball players and fans commonly believed that it was possible to throw a rising fastball—a pitch that would curve upward or hop as it approached the batter. This could be done, it was thought, by gripping the baseball across the seams and releasing the pitch with a wrist snap that would impart a pronounced backspin on the ball. Although they could not explain why it happened, pitchers, batters, and catchers were convinced that if the pitch was thrown at high speed—more than 90 mph—it would rise as it crossed the plate, causing the batter to misjudge the trajectory and swing under the ball. They were certain the ball rose because they could see it rise.

As a longtime baseball fan and a physicist specializing in the physics of sports, I was curious to find out whether the rising fastball was real. After all, a baseball must obey the laws of physics, and there was a well-established theory and sufficient data available to

>>>

allow me to calculate the aerodynamic forces on a baseball in flight. The basic principles are relatively simple. After the ball leaves the pitcher's hand, it is subject to just three forces: gravity (equal to the weight of the ball) pulling it vertically downward; aerodynamic drag, created by the collision of the ball with the surrounding air, which reduces its forward speed; and what is known as the Magnus force, which is generated by the interaction of the spinning surface of the ball with the air.

The ball generates a low-pressure wake behind it as it moves through the air, but if the surface is spinning, the wake is deflected sideways. According to Newton's law of action and reaction, if the ball deflects the air to one side, the air will push the ball in the opposite direction. The Magnus force always acts perpendicular to the path of the ball, deflecting it sideways according to the direction of spin. It is this force that allows pitchers to throw a repertoire of breaking balls—curveballs, sliders, sinkers, etc.—by adjusting the rate and direction of the spin on the

ball along with the speed and location of the pitch. To throw a rising fastball, the Magnus force must be directed upward, opposing the pull of gravity, and this can be achieved by throwing the ball with backspin. If the Magnus force is greater than the weight of the ball, then the net force on the ball will cause it to rise.

When I ran computer simulations of pitches, I made some interesting discoveries. I learned that over the standard pitching distance of 60 feet 6 inches, a ball loses about 9 percent of its initial speed due to aerodynamic drag—thus, a pitch launched at 90 mph will have slowed to 81 mph when it reaches the batter. The pitch takes only about 0.44 seconds to cover the distance. During this interval the ball falls about three feet due to the pull of gravity. A batter has less

than half a second to judge the trajectory of the ball, decide whether to swing, and then bring his bat around to the projected point of contact.

Hitting a baseball at the major-league level, I discovered, is a truly remarkable feat. Most significantly, I discovered that in order for the ball to truly rise in flight—for the Magnus force to exceed the weight of the ball—the pitch would have to be launched with a backspin of more than 3,600 rpm. This is far beyond the capacity of any major-league pitcher. High-speed photography shows that spin rates of about 1,800 rpm are the best that can be achieved. Thus, it is not humanly possible to throw a true rising fastball. With the ball spinning at 1,800 rpm and traveling at 90 mph, the Magnus force retards the vertical drop by a little more than a foot.

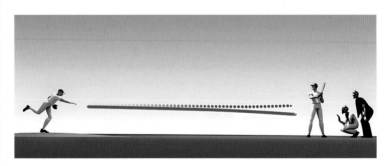

Pitchers, batters, and catchers swear that a ball can rise at the plate.

Instead of dropping three feet vertically on its way to the plate, the ball drops slightly less than two feet. I concluded that the rising fastball is an optical illusion. The ball appears to rise only because it doesn't fall as much as the batter expects it to—in other words, the ball rises only in relation to the batter's expectations. To the exquisitely trained eyes of a top-flight batter or catcher, the ball appears to rise because it does not fall as much as it would without the backspin.

Over time, a number of other scientists have verified my results. The most convincing confirmation has come from real-time tracking of baseball pitches using multiple video cameras and rapid computerized reconstruction of the trajectories. To the best of my knowledge, no one has ever recorded a fastball rising as it crosses the plate.

THE CATCHER TRADES IN A MASK FOR A HELMET

Why do baseball catchers now look like goalies on a hockey team? Blame it on Canada. Charlie O'Brien, at that time a catcher for the Toronto Blue Jays, was watching a hockey game and was struck how goalies simply shrugged off puck hits to their helmet. After working with Van Velden Mask Inc. and Major League Baseball, O'Brien developed a catcher's helmet called the All-Star MVP that was approved by Major League Baseball in 1996 and has since caught on everywhere.

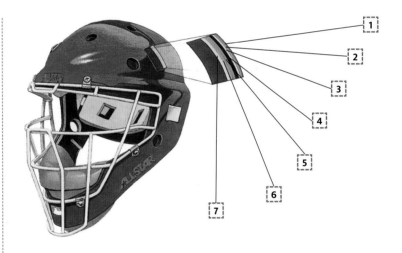

The All-Star MVP helmet is composed of seven layers. From the outside in:

1. Gelcoat **2.** 102-strand fiberglass **3.** Woven roving **4.** Kevlar
5. Kevlar **6.** 102-strand fiberglass **7.** Fine-mesh boat cloth

THE BREAKING PITCH

by JIM KAAT

This article was published in
POPULAR MECHANICS in 1997.

IT IS GAME 3 OF THE 1996 WORLD SERIES. THE ATLANTA BRAVES HAVE ALREADY TAKEN THE FIRST TWO GAMES IN THE BRONX. IF THEY CAN BEAT THE YANKEES IN ATLANTA'S FULTON COUNTY STADIUM, THEY'LL HOLD A SEEMINGLY INSURMOUNTABLE 3–0 LEAD IN THE SERIES, AND THE YANKEES CAN HANG IT UP UNTIL NEXT YEAR.

As a major-league pitcher for 25 years (1959–1983), left-hander Jim Kaat won 283 games and earned sixteen Gold Glove Awards.

But things have gone the Yankees' way in this game. A courageous effort by starting pitcher David Cone and excellent support by relievers Mariano Rivera and Graeme Lloyd have kept the Braves' big bats in check, and going into the bottom of the ninth, it is 5–2 Yankees as ace reliever John Wetteland takes the mound.

Wetteland is known for his blazing 99-mph fastball, and there is no reason for first batter Javier Lopez to look for anything else. Sure enough, Wetteland feeds Lopez nothing but heat, and all Lopez can do is ground feebly to Derek Jeter at short. But in his haste to make the play, Jeter bobbles the ball and Lopez is on.

Andruw Jones comes up. Jones, a rookie, has fed on Yankee pitching the first two games of the Series, including a couple of homers. A home run here and Atlanta is within one.

Wetteland bears down and brings heat. Jones looks at fastball after fastball, managing to foul a couple off and take a couple of balls. With the count two and two, Jones gears up for yet another fastball as Wetteland comes set and checks the runner. At almost 100 mph, Wetteland's fastball reaches home plate in less than half a second. Jones will have to start his swing before Wetteland actually releases the ball if he is to have any hope whatsoever of hitting it.

Wettleland deals. Jones starts his bat and begins to stride. The ball is released. But wait. Jones recognizes the spin on the ball. He sees the stitches. Oh, no! It isn't a fastball. It's a breaking ball. Jones tries to hold back his swing. His front leg has started to move. He holds back mightily. His left knee visibly buckles, but he holds back. He can't pull the trigger. His only hope is that the pitch will be called a ball.

"Steeeeh!" screams plate umpire Tim Welke.

Strike three.

Such is the power of the unexpected breaking pitch in baseball, especially when a power pitcher like John Wetteland sets it up with one fastball after another. In fact, in this game the next batter, Jeff Blauser, strikes out on three straight fastballs and pinch hitter Terry Pendleton grounds weakly to second to end the game. Knowing that Wetteland can throw a breaking ball at any moment is a weapon in itself. It throws off the batter's timing and prevents a hitter from merely sitting on a pitcher's fastball.

The breaking pitch—curveball, split-finger, slurve, slider, and other variations—has been around since baseball began. But never have so many pitchers thrown so many different breaking pitches with so many different looks as today. Pity the poor batter who has to decide what he is going to do with any given pitch in less than the one second it takes for the ball to leave the pitcher's hand and reach the hitting zone.

At one time, a batter could look for a fastball but was able to adjust to a breaking pitch that started out wide of the strike zone and then broke over the plate, or a breaking pitch that started high off the strike zone and broke down into it. Today, most breaking pitches move only an inch or two within the strike zone. And that's all it takes to cause a batter to miss or to hit the ball feebly. And today, breaking pitches move left, right, down, diagonally, and with variations on all of the above.

For years, the questions were whether a breaking pitch actually curved or whether it was just an optical illusion, or even simply a matter of trajectory. But now, with the availability of laser-based, computerized optical systems, it has been proven that the ball actually changes its flight path on the way to home plate.

As a former major-league pitcher, I threw thousands of breaking balls in my career. Frankly, I don't know why any of them curved as they left my hand. What I can tell you is that I can make a ball curve, slide, break, or drop. Much of the movement of the ball is controlled by the way it is gripped and released.

MECHANICS OF THE BREAKING PITCH

Breaking pitches spin, which results from applying finger pressure to the ball and snapping your wrist when releasing it. You'll get maximum spin by gripping the ball deeply within the fingers so that they wrap entirely around the ball, but your thumb has to be relaxed. I had an exercise I did when I was coaching pitchers. I'd say, "Squeeze the ball as tight as you can with your thumb and move your wrist." It didn't move very easily. But if you curl your fingers around the ball and barely lay your thumb on it, your entire wrist loosens up so you can snap it to get maximum spin.

The other element in a fast breaking pitch, such as the slider, is velocity. The key here is to stay behind the ball until the last possible second. Then, apply the wrist action for the particular pitch you're throwing. If you start rotating your wrist too early in the pitch, you lose velocity and get a slower, sloppier spin.

Sinking fastball: Sidespin and backspin are generated by fingertip pressure with either the index or middle finger on the seam when the ball is released.

Curveball: The palm is turned inward with a release as if you're pulling down on the ball. Sidespin and backspin should be imparted with the wrist, not the elbow.

Screwball: The palm is turned out on the release, and the ball breaks to the outside against right-handed hitters. Velocity is slower than that of a curveball.

While no two hurlers have exactly the same style of pitching, all of them strive for a consistent delivery in terms of arm angle and release point. The batter draws an imaginary rectangular box right where the pitcher releases the ball, and he looks for clues in that area as to what type of pitch will be coming at him. If the pitcher drops his arm a bit when he delivers a curveball, for instance, the batter will pick up on this and know when to expect a curve. Snapping the wrist on the release should happen so quickly that the batter can't pick up on it early in the delivery. Good hitters say they can recognize the curveball when it gets a particular distance from home plate. It happens so fast that they can't really see it until the ball gets close to home plate. They used to say Ted Williams could pick up a pitch right out of the hand. I don't think anyone can pick it up that quickly.

SINKING FASTBALL

(Pictured on the opposite page.) Looking at specific breaking pitches, the two-seam fastball, also called a moving or sinking fastball, is gripped on the top of the ball with the narrow seams exposed. This is in contrast to the four-seam fastball, which must be gripped on the wide seams to get it to travel in a true trajectory with all seams rotating. Both of these pitches are released with backspin.

When releasing this fastball, you usually apply pressure against the seam with either the index or middle finger. It's a matter of preference. This imparts the sidespin that causes the ball to drop.

CURVEBALL

Years ago, this pitch was called a drop. I throw a curve with a twelve o'clock to six o'clock rotation. This release imparts sidespin and backspin because I maintain pressure on the ball with my middle finger while rolling it over the top of my index finger. I like to throw the ball into the wind because this increases the ball's rotation and helps the break. The key to the curveball is to keep your hand behind the ball as long as possible, impart the spin with the wrist and not with the elbow, and make sure the thumb is relaxed. I shorten my stride by one inch or so, compared to pitching a fastball. The object here is not to be throwing the ball toward the batter. You want a feeling as if you're pulling down on the ball, almost as if you're throwing it into the ground. This type of motion gives the ball the desired trajectory.

SCREWBALL

The screwball is actually the opposite of the curveball in terms of snapping the wrist. Whereas I grip and release the ball with my

Forkball: Also called the splitter, the ball is released with a lot of velocity but with a tumbling rotation for a dramatic drop at the plate.

Slider: Releasing the ball off the index finger also imparts backspin and sidespin, causing lateral and downward movement.

palm turned inward for the curve, I turn my palm out when I'm throwing a screwball—almost as if I'm turning a screwdriver.

The ball's trajectory is similar to a curve, but it can't be thrown quite as hard. So the velocity is less than that of a curveball. Also, the ball breaks outward instead of inward. Left-handed pitchers like to throw screwballs to right-handed hitters because the ball starts toward the middle of the plate and then breaks away to the outside corner.

FORKBALL

The forkball, also known as the splitter, is an interesting pitch. You jam the ball between your first two fingers as hard as you can and you deliver it with the same action as a fastball, with the wrist coming straight over from the 12 to 6 o'clock position. The ball travels with a lot of velocity but with a tumbling kind of rotation. The rotation slows down as the ball approaches the plate, and if delivered correctly, the bottom kind of falls out of it.

SLIDER

The hard slider or short curve, as I used to call it, has a certain amount of lateral break and a certain amount of down break. It's a faster pitch than a curve, but it's slower than a fastball, and it has a shorter break than a curveball. If you judged the pitch by mph, and a pitcher's fastball is, say, 90 mph, and his curveball is 80 mph, he would want the slider to be in the 86-to-87-mph range. The harder you throw a slider, the shorter and quicker break you can get on it. The release technique is between a curve and a fastball.

Some pitchers release the ball off their middle finger. I throw my slider off my index finger. I try to feel as if I'm wiping over the outside of the ball as I snap on it in order to give it some backspin and sidespin.

OTHER VARIATIONS

A lot of pitchers today throw a slurve. They pitch the slider as if they are throwing a curve, and the ball comes out in a big, sweeping flat curve. I consider this pitch to be just a rather sloppy slider. It has a much wider break than the slider was intended to have, and I think this is one of the reasons there are so many more home runs today than years ago. Pitchers like Tom Seaver of the New York Mets could throw a true slider, whereas pitchers today would call that a cut fastball. A true slider breaks late and moves three or four inches—sort of a little slide. A true slider should be more of a power pitch. Pitchers today use the slider more as a breaking ball or an off-speed pitch.

Of all my pitches, the one that brings up the fondest memory is the slider. I remember a game in the late 1960s when I threw a really hard slider down and away to strike out Red Sox slugger Carl Yastrzemski to end the game with men on. Striking out Carl was pretty hard to do. I remember seeing that ball break. I threw a similar pitch to Don Zimmer in 1965, when I was playing for the Minnesota Twins, for the last out against the Washington Senators to clinch the pennant. When the ball comes out of your hand, you can almost feel whether it's going to have a good break or a little slip to it. Both of those balls felt really crisp coming out, and they both broke in the same spot. I still remember that distinctly. I wonder if Yastrzemski and Zim do?

THE PHYSICS OF A CURVEBALL

by PETER BRANCAZIO

For years, many scientists believed that the curveball was an optical illusion. As we shall see, this is not true. In fact, physicists have long been aware of the fact that a spinning ball curves in flight, going back to Sir Isaac Newton, who wrote a paper on the subject in 1671.

In 1852, the German physicist Gustav Magnus revived the topic when he demonstrated in an experiment that when a spinning object moves through a fluid, it experiences a sideways force. This phenomenon, now known as the Magnus effect, is the fundamental principle behind the curved flight of any spinning ball.

THE MAGNUS EFFECT
The theory of the Magnus effect is a relatively simple exercise in aerodynamics. When any object is moving through the air, its surface interacts with a thin layer of air known as the boundary layer. In the case of a sphere, which has a very poor aerodynamic shape, the air in the boundary layers peels away from the surface, creating a "wake"

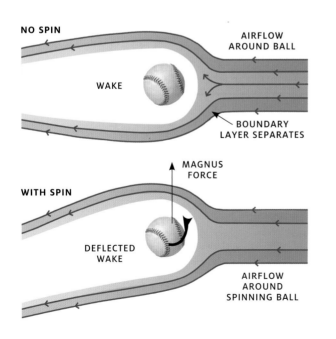

NO SPIN

AIRFLOW AROUND BALL

WAKE

BOUNDARY LAYER SEPARATES

MAGNUS FORCE

WITH SPIN

DEFLECTED WAKE

AIRFLOW AROUND SPINNING BALL

>>>

or lower-pressure region behind the ball. The front-to-back pressure difference creates a backward force on the ball, which slows its forward motion. This is the normal air resistance, or aerodynamic drag, that acts on any object moving through the air. However, if the sphere is spinning as it moves, the boundary layer separates at different points on opposite sides of the ball—further upstream on the side of the ball that is turning into the airflow, and further downstream on the side of the ball turning backward. As a consequence, the air flowing around the ball is deflected slightly sideways, resulting in an asymmetrical wake behind the ball. The effect is to generate a pressure difference across the ball, creating a lateral force component that pushes the ball sideways. This lateral force, at right angles to the forward motion of the ball, is known as the Magnus force.

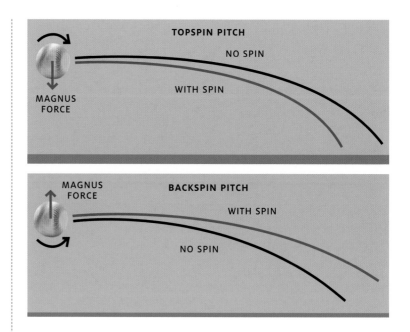

THE MAGNUS FORCE
The strength of the Magnus force is in direct proportion to the rate of spin as well as the forward speed of the ball—the greater the forward speed, the greater the force. It will also be proportional to the air density, which means that a ball will tend to curve less at higher altitudes where the air is thinner—a boon to hitters in a high-altitude city like Denver. The stitches on the baseball also help increase the Magnus force—not only by increasing the thickness of the boundary layer, but also by providing a place for the pitcher to put his fingers so he can put more spin on the ball. It should be noted, however, that stitches are not required to make a ball curve. Even a smooth-surfaced table tennis ball will curve if it is given enough spin.

On the other hand, the direction of the Magnus force depends only on the direction of spin. As shown in the diagram above, the force is always directed toward the side of the ball that is turning backward. In other words, the Magnus force always points in the same direction that the front of the ball is turning.

DIRECTING THE BALL
By properly orienting the spin direction, a pitcher can make the Magnus force point in any direction—left, right, up, down, and so on. For example, the natural clockwise rotation of a right-hander's wrist creates a leftward force (from the pitcher's perspective) that causes the ball to curve

away from a right-handed batter. When thrown with three-quarters overhand motion, the same pitch will curve down and away from the batter. Conversely, a left-handed pitcher's natural wrist rotation (which is counterclockwise) causes the ball to curve left to right—that is, into a right-handed batter and away from a left-hander. In order for a right-handed pitcher to imitate this motion of throwing the pitch known as the screwball, he must turn his wrist counterclockwise as he releases the ball—an unnatural, uncomfortable motion that frequently leads to elbow trouble. Much of the strategy of baseball is a direct consequence of the fact that right-handers and left-handers throw different pitches, simply because of a quirk of human physiology that makes our hands rotate more easily in one direction than the other.

A ball can be made to curve in a vertical plane as well. In fact, the trajectory of any thrown pitch has a natural downward curvature due to the force of gravity. However, by changing the spin direction, a pitcher can increase or decrease the curvature. For example, when a ball is thrown with topspin, the Magnus force will act toward the ground,

causing it to curve more sharply. If the ball is thrown with backspin, the Magnus force will point away from the ground, causing the ball to curve less. The latter pitch produces what is often called a rising fastball. However, the laws of aerodynamics tell us that for a baseball to physically rise, (that is, curve upward) as it approaches the batter, the Magnus force would have to be greater than the weight of the ball—an impossible feat for any human. For a full explanation of science behind this pitch, see "The Myth of the Rising Fastball" on page 55.

It seems pretty clear that no right-minded physicist would ever argue that a curveball is an illusion. However, as with the case of the rising fastball, we will argue that the sharp break of a curveball is illusory. While many hitters often report that a good overhand curveball breaks so sharply that it looks as if it is falling off a table, the laws of aerodynamics clearly show that the Magnus force cannot suddenly increase in flight—as would be required for a sudden change in curvature—but can only get smaller as the spin and speed of the ball slow down. The explanation for this illusion has to do with

how the batter perceives the flight of the ball. The angular motion of the ball—that is, its apparent motion across a batter's field of vision—seems relatively slow at first, but then increases as the ball approaches. In fact, it has been demonstrated that the angular motion becomes so rapid that no batter could possibly move his head fast enough to keep his eye on the ball all the way. When a good curveball is thrown, the change in its angular motion becomes even more pronounced as it nears the batter, greatly enhancing the appearance of its natural curvature and giving the illusion of a sharp bend.

ANATOMY OF A KNUCKLEBALL

by WAYNE COFFEY

R.A. DICKEY OF THE TORONTO BLUE JAYS, THE ONLY KNUCKLEBALLER EVER TO WIN THE CY YOUNG AWARD, CAN THROW MULTIPLE KNUCKLERS USING THE SAME GRIP AND MOTION—AND WATCH EACH ONE BREAK DIFFERENTLY. HERE, WE EXPLORE THE PHYSICS OF THE PITCH AND DICKEY'S MECHANICS OF THROWING IT.

Illusion and Reality: Dickey has said that he perceives most of his knucklers as rotating forward and falling down and away from a right-handed batter; slow-motion footage shows random movement and slight sidespin in addition to overspin.

PINNING DOWN THE ELUSIVE KNUCKLER

"Even science has a hard time explaining why knuckleballs do the things they do," he says. "That's part of the allure of the pitch."

GRIP

Dickey digs into the leather with the nails of his index and middle fingers just behind the runway, where the ball's seams are closest together; he places his thumb and ring finger on the sides of the ball. He keeps his nails even with a fine-tooth glass file and strong with the nail-hardening product Trind. Nails are a vital stabilizing force, enabling Dickey to release the ball with almost no spin.

WINDUP

Dickey loads up energy by shifting his weight to his rear (right) foot, kicking up his left knee, and turning his torso clockwise. His motion is more deliberate and controlled than that of a "normal" pitcher.

STRIDE

Normal pitchers aim to generate maximum power by pushing hard off their back leg and hurtling laterally toward home plate. Dickey limits his leg push and keeps his body upright, turning until his shoulders are square to the plate. His step forward is short. "Economy and simplicity are what you're after with the knuckleball," he says.

RELEASE

As Dickey moves his arm forward in front of his body, he loosens his grip and lets the ball float off his fingertips with minimal rotational force. His knuckler can reach 84 mph, and it spins 180 degrees or less as it travels 60.5 feet.

PITCHING 1949

by AUBREY O.
COOKMAN JR.

Baseball comes cloaked in a mantle of history unlike any other sport. Names like Mantle, Mays, Koufax, and many others are the stuff of legend. As this article published in 1949 (originally titled "Taking A Lesson from Champion Pitchers") demonstrates, the names of the players may have changed, but the skills used by pitchers of the 1940s (Carl Hubbell, Early Wynn, and Bob Feller, to name just three) are as familiar now as they were then.

WHAT DOES IT TAKE TO BE A BIG-LEAGUE PITCHER? EXPERTS IN THE BEST POSITION TO OBSERVE, LIKE CATCHER JIM HEGAN OF THE WORLD CHAMPION CLEVELAND INDIANS, GENERALLY AGREE THAT SPEED AND CONTROL ARE THE BIGGEST FACTORS. THE GAME'S GREAT PITCHERS HAVE VARIED WIDELY IN SIZE, SHAPE, AND TEMPERAMENT, AND MANY WERE FAMOUS FOR A PARTICULAR KIND OF PITCH, BUT EVERY ONE HAD BETTER-THAN-AVERAGE SPEED AND FINE CONTROL.

Bob Lemon struck out 1,277 batters for the Cleveland Indians during the course of his career (1946–58).

MASTERING CONTROL

Hegan knows how star hurlers perform. He catches a Cleveland staff that has been called the best ever assembled on one team. Two of its members, Bob Lemon and Gene Bearden, were twenty-game winners last season. A third, Bobby Feller, with nearly 200 major-league victories and over 2,000 strikeouts to his credit, ranks as one of baseball's all-time greats. A government-timing device clocked Feller's fast one at 99.5 mph. Batters have a split second to decide whether or not to swing with the ball hurtling toward them from only 60 feet 6 inches away—the distance between the mound and home plate. But even with his natural speed, Feller couldn't climb to stardom until he mastered control.

Some pitchers laid the groundwork for good control as youngsters by throwing for hours at a time at stationary targets. Some would pitch stones or balls at a hole in the fence. Others have rigged up "picture frames" of canvas or poles, with a 17-inch-wide and 38- or 39-inch-high opening representing the strike zone for an average-size batter.

Reduced to its simplest explanation, pitching skill is the ability to throw consistently what the batter least expects or wants. Watching the pitchers work from Hegan's vantage point behind the plate, you get a better idea of the finesse that makes a champion.

GIVING AWAY THE PITCH

Deceiving sharp-eyed big leaguers takes grade-A performance at all times. In their constant duel of wits, the pitcher can't afford to give the batter any inkling as to what kind of a pitch he'll serve up. Coaches and rival players are watching him constantly for telltale signs. Unconscious mannerisms sometimes betray a rookie pitcher's intentions. George Earnshaw of the Philadelphia Athletics originally had a habit of scuffing the ground around the mound with his toe when catchers flashed the curve sign, while the call for a fastball brought no such response. Until corrected, it was like posting an announcement each time for the hitter.

Urban "Red" Faber of the Chicago White Sox, a famous spitball pitcher, would overdo preparations for the saliva-applying

Dizzy Dean is best remembered as leader of the St. Louis Cardinals' "Gas House Gang" in 1934 as he posted a record of 30 wins and seven losses.

operations when he was faking his favorite delivery. Opponents noting the exaggerated facial contortions could be reasonably sure Faber's wicked "spitter" wasn't shortly coming their way. Babe Ruth, in his youthful pitching days, would unconsciously stick out his tongue when preparing to throw a curve. Others have unknowingly tipped off rivals by hitching up their shoulders prior to a certain type pitch, or crooking their wrist significantly during the start of the windup.

Managers and coaches are always on the alert to detect and correct these faults in their players. Occasionally a cagey pitcher will use these "giveaways" to his advantage in double-crossing rivals. Dizzy Dean (St. Louis Cardinals, Chicago Cubs, and St. Louis Browns, 1930–47) used to allow the opposition to "discover" his preliminaries for a certain type pitch, adding to its authenticity by using it a few times in the expected manner, then crossing them up at crucial moments by switching at the last minute to a completely different kind of pitch.

Coaches teach youngsters to deliver all pitches with the same motion, generally a three-quarter style, about midway between sidearm and overhand. Except for a few freak specialty pitches, the fingering—the way the ball is gripped—is basically the same for all pitches. A smart pitcher masks the fingering with his gloved hand. For about 75 percent of all pitches, the forefinger and second finger are on top of the ball, the thumb is below it, and the two remaining fingers fold down against the palm. Most experts advocate gripping the ball across the seams, rather than with them, to get better control.

TYPES OF PITCHES

A fastball behaves differently from a curve because of the way the ball is released. There isn't time then for a batter to react to the knowledge, even if he had it. Fastballs leave the hand with a downward snap of the wrist. A good, "live" pitch, in baseball parlance, seems to shoot upward when it nears the batter. One that comes straight and level across the plate is easy to hit, despite its speed, and it travels farther than breaking-type pitches.

Though held the same, a curve is thrown with an outward snap of the wrist so that the back of the pitcher's hand ends up facing the plate. The ball rolls off the first two fingers. Most effective curveballers put pressure on the second finger, just before the release, and use the first solely as a guide. The ball has to be made to spin in order to curve.

Some hurlers finger a slow ball, or "change up," just as they do a fastball or curve, but lift the top two fingers just as the ball

Carl Hubbell led the New York Giants to three pennants in five years during the 1930s with a devastating screwball.

Bob Feller (1936–56) of the Cleveland Indians led the American League in strikeouts for seven years. For his career, Feller struck out 2,581 batters.

is released. When thrown with the same motion as a fast one—except for the last-second wrist snap—it throws a batter's timing off badly.

The sharpest change of pace in baseball today is the "blooper ball" thrown by Rip Sewell of Pittsburgh. It floats plateward so slowly that batters can see the ball's seams and it arches down to them from as high as twelve to fifteen feet, but Rip uses it sparingly, and hitters aren't able to adjust their timing for solid swings.

Among the most effective "extra" deliveries is the knuckler. Manager Lou Boudreau of Cleveland claims it is the most baffling ball his star Bearden throws. Bearden grips it with the nails of his first three fingers and the sphere sails up to the plate with virtually no spin, breaking downward. Some knucklers, like Dutch Leonard of the Chicago Cubs, hold it with two fingers on top, pressing the first joints against the ball.

Carl Hubbell, the former New York Giant southpaw, perfected a screwball that he held just like a curve. The difference was in the inward snap he gave the ball on release, ending up with his palm facing the batter. This spin made the ball act like a reverse curve.

Early Wynn, another Cleveland star, has a bothersome slider that he grips like a curve, but holds slightly off center, and throws with less wrist snap. It breaks several inches but, unlike the curve, it "slides" away from right-handed batters without breaking downward.

USING YOUR RESOURCES

Some of the more methodical hurlers keep notebooks in which they jot down the data on the batting strengths and weaknesses of rivals. When a hitter like Rudy York (277 home runs over a thirteen-year career with the Detroit Tigers, Boston Red Sox, Chicago White Sox, and Philadelphia Athletics, 1934–48) displays a liking for pitches that catch the outside edge of the plate, it is pretty certain he'll never get one there when the game is close. Hurlers have equally long memories for weak points. Feller, who has been playing against Joe DiMaggio for ten years, thinks the Yankee star normally does the least damage to a ball that breaks low, on the outside corner.

Catchers are important to pitchers in analyzing the batter's stance and swing. This is particularly true when a newcomer is at bat. If he is a plate-crowder, the catcher will probably call for balls that break in close to his bat handle. Or, if he stands too far back, the catcher might ask for a curve or a fastball that nicks the corner.

FOUL BALL! TRICKY PITCHES, FREAKY BATS

by JIM KAAT

This article was published in POPULAR MECHANICS in 1988.

FOR ALL THE WRONG REASONS, 1987 WAS ONE OF THE MORE MEMORABLE SEASONS IN BASEBALL. THREE PLAYERS WERE PENALIZED FOR A DUBIOUS SORT OF ACHIEVEMENT. THESE PLAYERS WERE PENALIZED UNDER THE RULES THAT PROHIBIT THE DEFACING OF BALLS OR THE USE OF FREAK BATS. THAT RULE—AGAINST PITCHING A BALL THAT HAS BEEN ROUGHENED, WET, POLISHED, OR OTHERWISE TAMPERED WITH—ENTERED THE BOOKS IN 1920.

The Toronto Blue Jays' R. A. Dickey is the only active player in the majors who uses the knuckleball as his primary pitch.

Through 1980, a period of 60 years, only two pitchers had ever been disciplined. That number was matched in 1987 when Joe Niekro of the Minnesota Twins and Kevin Gross of the Philadelphia Phillies each received a ten-day suspension for bringing to the mound an abrasive that might be used to scuff the ball—sandpaper in the case of Gross, an emery board in the case of Niekro. And when a bat shattered in the hands of Houston's Billy Hatcher on the night of September 1 and was found to contain cork, Hatcher got an involuntary vacation with pay and his manager got to pay a fine.

There's no doubt that the subjects of illegal pitches and doctored bats received more attention in 1987 than any season before, despite the fact that they had to share the limelight with questions about the allegedly livelier ball.

From my perspective in the broadcast booth, from talking to players off-camera, and from my own experience in the game, I believe that the percentage of pitchers and batters who break the rules on a consistent basis is actually very small. At the same time, I believe that because of certain changes in the game over the past twenty years or so, there is probably a greater tendency and temptation today to look for an edge, whether it is a legal one, like the split-fingered fastball, or illegally trying to simulate the splitter's movement by loading the ball.

THE BATTER'S ADVANTAGE

It's a fact that batters are muscling up, swinging lighter bats, and swinging them more aggressively. And why not? The effective strike zone is smaller than ever before, so a pitcher really has a tougher time keeping the ball off the fat of the bat.

What the pitchers are throwing, from amateur ball to the majors, is more off-speed stuff and breaking balls, including the split-fingered fastball. Fewer pitchers are challenging the batter with natural, live, trust-your-stuff fastballs, especially during the late innings of a close game. Have you noticed the inordinate number of late-inning, often game-winning home runs hit off a breaking ball? That kind of pitch loses its crispness when the thrower gets arm-weary, and it tends to hang. The same goes for

When umps nabbed Twins pitcher Joe Niekro with an emery board in the summer of 1987, he was suspended.

split-fingered fastballs, scuffballs, and even sliders, although these take their toll in swinging third strikes too, especially with more batters swinging wildly instead of merely trying to make contact.

Speaking of the fences, they keep getting closer and closer in today's ballparks. Besides these factors, higher temperatures and humidity can turn a few fly balls into home runs. Dr. Robert Watts, a mechanical engineer at Tulane University, actually computed how far a ball will travel on a hot, humid day compared to a cool, dry one. Watts says that a ball might carry twenty feet farther under warm, moist conditions, where the air density actually decreases, thereby exerting less drag.

A DIFFERENT BALL?

All the talk about trick pitches, corked bats, livelier balls, and whatnot in 1987 sparked a good deal of research and speculation in many science labs all around the country. The belief was widespread among baseball professionals that the ball was livelier in 1987 than in 1986. I believe so myself, from the miracles I've seen flying out of places that are not hitters' ballparks.

Nonetheless, the leagues conducted lab tests around mid-season and announced that the ball's coefficient of restitution—a measurement of how well (or how poorly) the ball bounces back upon hitting a hard surface—was no different than in 1986. After being fired by machine and colliding at an initial velocity of 85 feet per second—58 mph—a major-league baseball must show a coefficient of restitution between 51.4 and 57.8 percent. If it's any higher, the ball is too lively. If it's any lower, it's something only a pitcher could love. The size and weight of the balls were also within the tolerances permitted.

If the 1987 ball didn't have more hop, then another ball-related factor might account for why so many missiles went into orbit. Dr. Joel Hollenberg, of the prestigious Cooper Union engineering school in New York, speculates that the stitches might impart some extra mileage. Since the early 1980s, Hollenberg has studied the aerodynamic forces that cause the knuckleball to behave in its erratic fashion. His research shows that the knuckler's shifting sideways motion is determined by the orientation of the ball's stitches against the airflow as the pitch travels to the plate.

In 1987, Hollenberg reran some of his 1983 experiments, but with 1987 major-league balls. His data on drag kept coming out differently. The only variable, he realized, could be a different texture to the stitches. After repeated tests the evidence just stared him in the face: he describes the stitching as rougher, or more pronounced. Others have noticed the 1987 ball's stitching seemed slightly more raised than usual. That type of ball is usually a pitcher's delight.

Besides the number of stitches and type of string, the major-league specifications aren't too specific about stitching. If they are higher, this means the shape of the ball is rougher—uniformly round but nor uniformly smooth. You might be surprised to learn that Hollenberg and others state that a rough sphere is more aerodynamic than a smooth one. This is the secret behind the golf ball, with its 336 dimples. It seems that the roughness creates a more turbulent airflow around the ball, which has the effect of breaking up or reducing the ball's wake. The invisible wake exerts drag on the ball. But if the wake is reduced, the ball travels farther.

A somewhat related hypothesis, from Dr. Peter Brancazio of Brooklyn College's Physics Department, contends that a scuff on the ball might play a similar role in reducing drag. Brancazio and others point out that this would depend upon the ball's rate of spin, the degree of scuffing, and the position of the scuff in relation to the ball's direction of spin.

You'll rarely find a scofflaw who admits to it while he's an active player, as did Gaylord Perry and Bill "Spaceman" Lee. But the list of felons who've confessed after retirement includes Whitey Ford, Jim Brosnan, George Bamberger, and the angelic-sounding duo of Schoolboy Rowe and Preacher Roe. Even Bill Kunkel, the American League umpire and former pitcher, once indicated he could detect a spitball from hands-on experience.

SPITBALLS

To make what is commonly called a spitball effective, the pitcher must make the surface of the ball as smooth as possible in the area where he will grip it, which is on the covers, never the seams. The object is to eliminate friction in the grip so that the ball has no rotation or spin when it's released.

Preparing the smooth surface can be accomplished by the wet or dry method. The ball can be moistened with saliva, which can become a little slicker when the ball-doctor chews lozenges made from the bark of the slippery elm tree. More up-to-date pharmaceuticals include lubricants such as K-Y Jelly and petroleum jelly. Soap will do the trick too. Usually, these substances are smeared on the pitcher's skin, hair, or uniform, and they're difficult for an umpire to detect.

The dry spitter can be prepared with powdery materials. Talcum will work. And I clearly recall that the mound in Cleveland has fine, filmy dirt that's perfect for the task. Getting some on your finger is literally as easy as tying your shoes.

Wet-head or dry-look, the spitter is thrown with the same motion and velocity as the fastball. But when it's released—and it virtually squirts out between the fingers, as a Ping-Pong ball would if you pinched it—it has none of the fast rotation that a pitcher would usually want on a pitch. As a result, the ball meets air resistance and suddenly, very suddenly, loses velocity and drops straight down.

SCUFFBALLS

With scuffballs and cut balls the break is sideways, left or right. Either way, the break comes late—after the batter has judged where the ball will be. Here, you want to generate friction with the ball, and that's what abrasion achieves.

The pitch is thrown with a fastball grip, fastball delivery, and usually at fastball speed. The way a pitcher grips his fastball determines where the ball gets scuffed. But to break sideways, the scuff must remain the same spot, perpendicular to the direction of the pitch as the ball spins bottom over top toward the plate.

Because the ball is rougher on one side, that spot creates turbulence in that air that flows over it on the way home. As Watts and others explain, the turbulent air peels away from the rough spot, making the air's wake shift around the smoother side of the ball. This causes an imbalance that redirects the airflow and forces the ball to veer to the scuffed side.

If science has demystified what the scuff does to the ball, how it gets on the ball remains a total mystery to any pitcher who has ever been confronted by an umpire.

Of course, baseballs do get nicked and scratched in the normal course of duty. A foul off the backstop or a sharp grounder, especially on artificial turf, will leave scars. That's found money. The man-made variety takes more ingenuity.

In the days when most uniforms had belts, some pitchers might sharpen the buckle so they could cut shallow grooves in the ball while contemplating signs from the catcher. Double knits banished the buckle, but resourceful pitchers might conceal a needle, tack, or other sharp object beneath a bandage on his glove hand and give the ball a rough shave while he's rubbing it up.

As for scuffing, any abrasive substance will do. New York Yankees pitcher Whitey Ford has related how he wore a ring that was filigreed to the texture of a wood rasp. Sandpaper, emery cloth, and emery boards have found their way to the mound from the hardware store and manicure parlor. A roughened spot about the size of a quarter is all the scuff you need.

But ball needn't be cut or scuffed to have a sudden break. Even a splotch of mud will create the same aerodynamic irregularities. And it needn't be the pitcher who doctors the ball. Ford had his famous mudball prepared for him courtesy of catcher Elston Howard. Additionally, catchers have been known to scrape the ball against their shin guards, and certain Dodgers infielders of the 1960s were suspected of cutting the ball for certain Dodgers pitchers as it was tossed around the bases.

CORKED BATS

With all these trick deliveries in the pitcher's arsenal, not to mention the legal stuff, you would think the use of corked bats, as alleged, would be justifiable self-defense for batters.

I don't think that corked bats are used as a conscious counterweight to the perception that a pitcher might be doctoring the ball. It's merely an attempt by the batter to improve his performance, satisfy his ambitions, or solve his problems. For the guy with TP, or track power—the ability to hit fly balls out to the warning track—a corked bat might mean several more home runs.

This is to the extent that corked bats are used at all—and I don't believe the practice is widespread. The only major leaguer I know of who was candid about the fact was the late Norm Cash, who said he used a corked bat when he played for the Detroit Tigers in 1961 and won the American League batting title with a .361 average and 41 home runs.

There's a lot of voodoo involved with freak bats, both regarding how to load one and what the loading is supposed to achieve. From the woodworking angle, the magical formulas vary but are basically as follows.

A hole anywhere from 1 to $1\frac{1}{2}$ inches in diameter is bored through the fat end of the bat to a depth of about 1 foot. The wood that's been removed is replaced by cork (a dowel, beads, or rolled sheets) or bouncy Super Balls press-fit into the hollow barrel. Finally, the mouth of the hole is plugged with wood that matches the grain, and the top of the bat is stained and finished in a manner that camouflages the plug.

Why does anyone load a bat? One reason is to lighten it and thereby generate greater bat speed—the force with which the bat meets the ball. Another reason is bat control. If it takes less effort to bring the bat around, the hitter gains an extra fraction of a second to gauge the pitch before he commits to swinging.

Another thing some players believe is that the cork or rubber filling endows the bat with greater resiliency, making the ball jump off the bat with more pop. But science says it isn't so.

Los Angeles Dodgers player Wilton Guerrero was ejected from the game at St. Louis in the first inning on June 1, 1997, after breaking his bat on a groundout to second base. Dodgers manager Bill Russell (left) is shown the bat by home-plate umpire Thomas Rippley (right) as third-base umpire Bruce Froemming (center) looks on. It was found that the bat had been corked. Guerrero later admitted that the bat had been doctored. The Dodgers beat the Cardinals 6–1.

Lighter weight, not resiliency, is what makes the freak bat drive the ball farther. As Brancazio and others explain, the bat hardly deforms at all when it collides with the ball—or only hundredths of an inch if at all. But upon collisions, the ball deforms by an inch or two, squishing down almost to a hemisphere. So whatever you fill the bat with doesn't matter, as long as it is lighter than wood. And cork, according to Brancazio, has about one-third the density of wood. Super Balls give almost no weight savings at all. But something stiff and light like Styrofoam would work well too. Actually, a hollow bat would work best—if the hitter could be confident that the bat would hold up and not sound too hollow to the nearby catcher and umpire. In fact, Brancazio says that the newer-style cupped bats, the ones with an inch-deep scoop of wood removed from the business end, achieve the same effect in bat speed as boring out several cubic inches of wood farther down the barrel. That's because the mass, or weight, is removed farther away from the bat's pivot point at the handle. The net result is a lower polar moment of inertia when the hitter begins to swing.

What's the net result on the scoreboard? In his Tulane University lab, Watts has calculated that a hitter using a 32-ounce bat generates a bat speed of about 70 mph. If termites or other activity shed six ounces from this weight, bat speed rises about 2.5 percent to about 72 mph. The extra velocity, says Watt, translates into fifteen to twenty feet more mileage for the ball if it collides with the bat.

BACKSPIN IN A HIT

Meanwhile, another revelation from Watts's lab almost makes the point of corking the bat irrelevant. It has to do with the role of backspin in making a ball travel farther.

When a ball is propelled so the seams turn into the airflow, or against it, from the bottom of the ball to the top, it's said to have backspin. This orientation creates the force known in aerodynamics as lift. The more rpm in the spin, the greater the lifting force.

The way to give backspin to a batted ball is to undercut it with the swing. If you undercut the pitch too much, you pop up. Watts tells us that the optimal launch point is an area five-eighths to one inch below the equator of the ball. The difference between this uppercut and hitting the ball dead-center (so that it hardly spins) could, depending upon the angle of the swing, put as much as several thousand rpm of backspin on the ball—good for about 250 feet more travel. With just a small increase in backspin, the ball would travel another 30 feet.

Smart hitters have always sensed this, and Watts believes

that more batters are becoming savvy to it. He points out that the amount of backspin is affected by the amount of friction generated when the bat strikes the ball. Applying a substance such as pine tar to the hitting surface of the bat would increase friction, but this is illegal. Something players used to do years ago was scrape out the dark-grained areas of the wood—in effect scoring the bat's surface in a manner resembling the face of a golf club—where the grooves are intended to impart backspin to the ball.

Although scuffing and corking are called cheating, I don't agree with the term. Professional baseball players are more or less evenly matched. Everyone knows what is at stake, so I don't believe that taking an edge is cheating in the moral sense. Ballplayers call it gamesmanship.

All things being equal, I think the trick pitches and freak bats ought to be legal. After all, let's look at some practices that are never questioned, or just winked at, but which give someone an edge.

THE LEGAL ADVANTAGES

Home teams routinely groom the field to give themselves an advantage, or put visitors at a disadvantage. The baselines get beveled to make bunts go fair or foul. The area in front of the plate can be watered down to favor a sinkerball pitcher, or hardened to cause Baltimore chop–type infield hits. Teams regularly soak the base paths or dump sand around first base to slow down base stealers. There are no strictures against any of this in the rulebook. At the time when I played for the Minnesota Twins, the Chicago White Sox used to store the baseballs in a freezer to deaden the ball. When our power hitters made contact, it was like hitting a rock—the ball didn't go anywhere. While we're at it, let's not forget about stealing the signs, or the way hitters stand behind the boundary of the batter's box to get a longer look at the pitch, or how a first baseman plants a foot in foul territory when setting up for a pickoff throw. And how a New York team (Yankees) moved its fences closer to its batters.

All of these things fall into the category of getting an edge. It's not as though they're criminal acts. And no matter if the book says they're legal or not, I don't think we'll see any less of them in the years to come.

TOP TEN CORKERS

[1] **SAMMY SOSA,** Chicago Cubs. Caught on June 3, 2003. Places a shadow on the 600-plus home runs hit over his career.

[2] **NORM CASH,** Detroit Tigers. Confesses after his retirement to using a corked bat in 1961 when he hit 41 HRs and 132 RBIs and led the American League in batting with a .361 average.

[3] **AMOS OTIS,** Kansas City Royals. After retiring in 1984, the five-time All-Star admits to using a doctored bat through much of his career.

[4] **GRAIG NETTLES,** New York Yankees. On September 7, 1974, Super Balls pop out of his broken bat. Nettles is not punished, and his previous home run is allowed to stand as the Yanks win 1–0 over the Detroit Tigers.

[5] **ALBERT BELLE,** Cleveland Indians. On July 15, 1994, a suspicious umpire confiscates Belle's bat. After the game, a teammate switches bats, but the subterfuge is spotted and Belle gets a seven-game suspension.

[6] **CHRIS SABO,** Cincinnati Reds. On July 29, 1996, umpires catch Sabo with a corked bat, but he denies it is his bat. Sabo gets a seven-game suspension.

[7] **BILLY HATCHER,** Houston Astros. Nabbed on August 31, 1987. He claims to have borrowed the bat from a pitcher. Hatcher gets a ten-day suspension.

[8] **WILTON GUERRERO,** Los Angeles Dodgers. Caught June 1, 1997. Guerrero admits his guilt and gets an eight-game suspension.

[9] **MIGUEL OLIVIO,** catcher on Chicago White Sox double-A minor-league team. He gets a six-game suspension in 2001.

[10] **JOSE GUILLEN,** triple-A minor leaguer in Devil Rays system. Guillen admits error of his ways and gets a ten-game suspension in 2001.

Basketball

ANATOMY OF THE FREE THROW

by ALLISON T. McCANN

This article appeared in
POPULAR MECHANICS in 2012.

FRENZIED MARCH MADNESS BASKETBALL GAMES OFTEN COME DOWN TO A MADDENING EXCHANGE OF FREE THROWS. WE ASKED THE EXPERTS HOW TO GET THE MECHANICS AND ANGLES FOR A PERFECT FREE THROW. IN THEORY, THE FREE THROW IS A GIFT.

The shooter shoots with no elbows thrown in his direction, no seven-foot-tall man trying to block the shot, and no screaming crowd (unless he plays for the visiting team). So what makes this solo shot so choke-worthy? In the spirit of March Madness, we break down the anatomy of this seemingly simple shot.

BODY MECHANICS

"The lift that you have as a free-throw shooter starts from the feet," says Bruce Kreutzer, a shooting specialist at the Mark Price Basketball Academy in Suwanee, Georgia, who has been working with the NBA and amateur players for 25 years. "The majority of players today use their upper body first, which really throws off the rhythm."

When they step up to the line, players should align their body—toes, hips, and shoulders—directly with the basket, Kreutzer says. Seems easy enough, but things soon become complicated. The amount of bend in the knee needed to make a shot is directly proportional to a player's distance from the hoop, and players often struggle to find the amount of bend that correlates with the right amount of energy buildup. Too much energy and your shot is a brick off the backboard; not enough and it's an air ball.

As a player prepares to shoot, the ball should be resting on the finger pads (that first roll of knuckles just above your palms) and not the fingertips, Kreutzer says—"This way there's no snap, just a rhythmic flop." In the release, the shooting arm and support arm should extend toward the basket. The same goes for the rest of the body; the shooter's weight should be traveling forward in a controlled calf-raise motion.

DEBUNKING THE SWISH

North Carolina State University mechanical engineering professor Larry Silverberg, an avid baller himself, set out to determine the physics behind the perfect free throw. With his colleague Chau Tran, he co-wrote a software program to analyze three-dimensional computer-simulated free-throw trajectories.

"If you take top athletes in any sport, most have a really hard time explaining what they're doing," Silverberg says. "By

◀ Mark Price of the Cleveland Cavaliers sets up a free throw against the Milwaukee Bucks during an April 16, 1994 game.

simulating millions of shots we could see patterns that tend to confirm best practices."

Their extensive research allowed them to establish a few guidelines for the foul line: aim toward the back of the rim with 3 Hz of backspin and at 52 degrees to the horizontal. Oh, and do all this at a perfectly smooth and consistent speed.

Let's take the first piece of advice: Aim for the back of the rim. Despite what most people may think, Silverberg found that aiming for the center of the basket actually decreases the likelihood of a successful shot by almost 3 percent. Silverberg and Tran found that the sweet spot is actually 2.82 inches past the center of the hoop. You might make fewer "nothing but net" shots this way, as the ball is more likely to hit the back of the rim and go in, but your overall shooting percentage will be greater.

Second piece of advice: the backspin. Three Hz of backspin translates to three complete revolutions of the ball before it reaches the hoop, and the reason you want this backspin is that it deadens the ball, should it hit the rim or backboard during flight. In their simulations, Silverberg and Tran found no additional advantage to more than three revolutions; plus, they found that players struggle to put more backspin than this anyway.

Finally, the angle: Without a protractor in your sneakers, it might be difficult for players to execute a launch angle of exactly 52 degrees. The shorthand version that Silverberg tells players, then, is to shoot the ball so that it's about 2 inches below the top of the backboard at its highest point.

"Imagine you drew a line from where the ball is released to the hoop—that's the angle from the horizontal," he says. "A good way to visualize this is aiming pretty close to the top of the backboard at the top of [the ball's] trajectory."

Of course, this is a loose rule, in part because basketball players vary wildly in height. Silverberg and Tran came up with the 52 degrees rule for a six-foot-six player, so the angle would be different for a seven-foot center, a six-foot-six point guard, or a five-foot-eight insurance salesman playing with buddies on the weekend. But of all the parameters of the free throw, maintaining a constant speed is the most important but also the most difficult, Silverberg says. Unlike the geometric conditions, backspin and speed are variables that rely on the shooter's ability to maintain a consistent motion—arguably the most difficult aspect of any shot.

Football players watch endless game film; baseball players in a hitting slump head to the video room to see what's amiss with their swing. And basketball players can watch video of their free-throw attempts with a full statistical analysis of each shot. John Carter, CEO of Noah Basketball, is one of the people bringing big data to basketball. He developed a little device called Noah that analyzes the arc of the ball once it leaves a player's hands, computing its angle of entry into the basket and spitting out this number in real time so that shooters can adjust their arc accordingly. For a free throw, entry-angle perfection is around 43 degrees. And, unlike the launch angle, which varies with player height, the entry angle is the same for all shooters.

"If a player shoots flat, the hole closes up," Carter says. "There's a sweet spot in the mid forties where you can have a little bit of variation in the arc, but the ball goes in at almost the same distance from back of rim every time."

Noah devices have compiled statistics for thousands of free-throw shots, confirming what Silverberg's simulations showed. Even though an entry angle of about 50 degrees corresponds to a perfect swish, the Noah data showed that players' overall shooting percentage started to decrease at above 45 degrees. So great shooters hit the back of the rim more often than they swish.

NOTHING BUT NET: MAKING THE 3-POINT SHOT

by BUZZ "THE SHOT DOCTOR" BRAMAN

This article was published in POPULAR MECHANICS in 1994.

FOR A BASKETBALL PLAYER, THERE'S NO BETTER FEELING THAN SEEING A SHOT SWISH THROUGH THE BASKET. WHETHER IT'S AT THE BEGINNING OF THE GAME, AT THE BUZZER, OR FROM OUT IN 3-POINT LAND, MAKING BASKETS IS THE ESSENCE OF THE GAME.

To be a complete offensive player, a consistent jump shot is a must. Hot-and-cold shooting is a product of mechanical flaws in the stroke. In many respects, a 3-point shot is the same as a free throw since, mechanically, the shots are the same. The difference lies in the speed at which the shot is taken. A free throw is shot at whatever speed you want to shoot. A 3-pointer is shot at the speed the game dictates.

Shooting has become a lost art. In the past twenty years, the game has shifted toward athleticism. The National Basketball Association (NBA) and athletic shoe companies are marketing the dunk. Instead of practicing shooting, young players spend their time practicing the "slam." However, the growing importance of the 3-point shot—put up from 22 feet and beyond in the NBA—is now making good shooters a premium.

The NBA game has evolved into a game of double-teaming the superstar—someone like Shaquille O'Neal. When the ball is passed out of the double-team in the low post underneath the basket, the result is an open jump shot or an open 3-pointer. If more players could shoot the 3, there would be no more double-teaming. Zone defenses would be a thing of the past.

DIFFICULTIES OF THE 3-POINTER

So why is it so hard to shoot the 3-point shot?

The two biggest excuses for poor shooting are lack of confidence and lack of concentration. These are the standard answers given by coaches, players, and parents. What they don't realize is that lack of confidence and concentration are the effect, not the cause. When the ball doesn't go in, confidence and concentration slide.

But the real reason that the ball isn't going in consistently is poor mechanics. When the mechanics get straightened out and the ball starts going in the basket, guess what happens to a player's confidence and concentration?

All young players are taught several lessons about shooting that are important. You should "square up," meaning your shoulders and feet face the basket. You should also bend your knees for power and concentrate on the target.

Ray Allen of the Miami Heat shoots against the Boston Celtics at American Airlines Arena in Florida on October 30, 2012.

These things are important, but let's face it, these are things most players do naturally.

The two biggest reasons for poor shooting are not being able to make the ball go straight consistently and not being able to judge distance correctly. What does this mean? It's really very simple.

There are only four ways to miss a shot: left, right, short, or long. If you could shoot a 3-pointer using a computer, all you would need to do is draw a straight line from the middle of the release, your fingertips, to the middle of the rim, which would be adjusted for the correct amount of thrust and arc for the ball to go the correct distance.

To be a consistent shooter, you must understand how to shoot straight and how to accurately judge the distance to the basket. Otherwise, you're shooting by instinct, and this leads to streaky shooting.

PROPER HAND PLACEMENT

For simplicity's sake, let's assume everyone is right-handed. To start, hold out your arm fully extended and with your fingertips spread. Look down your forearm as though you were looking down the barrel of a rifle. If you draw a straight line down your forearm to your fingertips, you will notice that only two of your fingers are within that straight line: your index and middle fingers.

Now hold a ball in your right hand as if you were going to shoot the ball. The shape that is formed from your wrist to your elbow and from your elbow to your shoulder should look like an L. When you make the L, it should be brought in front of you so that the straight line created by your forearm and extending up to your index and middle fingers is lined up toward the middle of the basket.

The shooting motion is an exercise in simplicity. From the L position, we bend our knees, thereby lowering the L. Then we simply push up. When the ball rolls off the fingers, guess which two fingers touch the ball last?

That's right. It's the index and middle fingers. The very last finger that touches the ball is the index finger. The miracle of straightness is this: wherever your index finger points when you release the ball and follow through is where the ball goes. When you push up under the L, your elbow locks straight and your wrist breaks. If your index finger is pointed over the middle of the front rim, the ball will never miss right or left. Since the rim is a circle, you can always see the middle of the rim no matter what angle you shoot from.

1.

2.

3.

4.

5.

▲ **Shoot and Freeze:** The L-shaped shooting arm rises so the line from the forearm through the index and middle fingers lines up toward the basket. Freeze the follow-through until the ball reaches the basket.

1. The index and middle fingers of the shooting hand point toward the basket.

2. As the body elevates, the ball begins to roll off the fingers.

3. The left hand, fingers pointed upward, falls away from the ball.

4. Aim your index finger over the front of the rim and release the shot.

5. Follow through with the wrist bent over and fingers pointing downward.

Meanwhile, the correct amount of arc on the shot will be determined by three factors: the natural upward push motion of the L; your instincts; and freezing the follow-through at the point of release—when your arm locks straight and your wrist flips over—at a spot about six to eight inches above the rim.

So what is your other hand—the left hand in this instance—doing? Its job is very simple. A ball should be shot with only one hand. The left hand is just for support.

For a right-handed shooter, the left hand should be placed on the side of the ball at about the nine o'clock position. As the L moves forward, the left hand loses contact with the ball when the ball is level with your forehead. All five fingers of the left hand are straight up and down. The arm is bent and the palm faces to the right.

The left hand is not allowed to shoot, push, flick, twist, or face the basket. If it does, you are shooting with two hands.

What's so bad about shooting with two hands? If the palm of your left hand starts rotating toward the basket, then you are pushing the ball to the right and off the index and middle fingers. Remember, the ball goes where the index finger is pointing. Missing right or left is the result of the left hand pushing the ball. This is a very common mistake for players of all ages.

GOOD FOLLOW-THROUGH

Most players rely solely on their instincts and "feel" when it comes to judging distances. These are important considerations but not the only ones. The follow-through is a critical element as well. As it happens, follow-through is a phrase every basketball player has heard but which few can define.

The follow-through forms as the L of your arm rises, the arm locks straight, and, as the ball is released, the wrist finishes bent over with the fingertips pointing downward. After shooting the ball, you should freeze in this position like a statue, and don't move until the ball reaches the basket. This is the correct follow-through. When you have the same release and structure on every shot, you can then use your instincts and "feel" to a greater degree. Simply put, the method is shoot and freeze.

To better understand the importance of the follow-through, try this experiment. Stand at the foul line and, with the L formed, push up. As you shoot, jerk your arm back as fast as you can. You'll find you have no control over the ball.

Next, shoot and freeze. You now have maximum control over the direction of the ball.

"Pulling the string" is the phrase used to describe that jerking

Clutch Shot: Dallas Mavericks guard Steve Nash (right) launches a 3-point shot over Portland Trailblazers forward Dale Davis that proved to be the game winner of Game 2 in the NBA Western Conference quarterfinals at the American Airlines Center in Dallas, April 23, 2003. Note the follow-through.

motion of pulling your arm back before you've finished the follow-through. Imagine there is a string connecting your index finger to the ball.

PRACTICE, PRACTICE, PRACTICE

The high school and college 3-point shot is 19 feet 9 inches. I once did a shooting demonstration at Villanova University for the Philadelphia 76ers' coaching staff and about twenty rookies. I shot 250 college 3-pointers and made 246. I made the first 92 in a row. I could hear the players' amazement as I shot.

What they didn't realize was that my mechanics were perfect: a perfect L shape of the arm, a perfect shoot-and-freeze motion, and a perfect left-hand release. Every ball I shot went straight.

Of course, they also wanted to shoot 3-pointers like that. But something else they didn't realize was that I shot 300 3-pointers a day for six months, training for that exhibition. Don't think that you can practice shooting a 3-pointer, or any other shot for that matter, by shooting only a few shots per day.

Practice does not make perfect. Perfect practice makes perfect.

To master the 3-point shot or any other shot, you need to practice it so many times it becomes second nature. It must become ingrained in your mind. Muscle memory is the key to becoming a good shooter. Even if your team is down by 2 points and there is only 1.5 seconds left in the game, when you pull up for the 3—assuming your technique is correct and you've prepared with long hours of practice—the only sound you'll hear before the crowd begins to roar will be the sound of your 3-point shot swishing through the net.

SLAM DUNK!

by PETER BRANCAZIO

THE SLAM DUNK
INVARIABLY BRINGS
A BASKETBALL
CROWD ROARING TO
ITS FEET, AND, MORE
OFTEN THAN NOT,
THE PLAYER MAKING
THE SHOT WILL
FOLLOW
IT WITH A FIST PUMP
OR SOME OTHER
DISPLAY OF SELF-
CONGRATULATION.
BUT JUST HOW
IMPORTANT IS
THE SLAM DUNK
AS AN OFFENSIVE
WEAPON? IS IT GREAT
BASKETBALL OR
JUST SHOWMANSHIP?
HOW MUCH SKILL IS
REQUIRED TO BE A
SUCCESSFUL DUNKER?

The career achievements and leadership role of LeBron James during Miami Heat's 2012 and 2013 season catapulted him to the top of many Best of the NBA lists.

TYPES OF DUNKS

The scientific study of any phenomenon normally begins with the description and classifications of its forms. In this case, careful observation reveals that slam dunks actually fall into a relatively simple set of categories. The basic slam dunk begins with the shooter getting the ball on a pass or rebound within three feet of the basket, requiring, at most, one step to get to the hoop. The ball may be delivered one-handed or two-handed with varying degrees of force, ranging from a gentle dropped-in dunk to a resounding two-handed overhead slam.

The next level of dunkmanship is the alley-oop. In this play, the player catches a pass in midair above the rim and jams it home. Requiring unspoken communication between passer and receiver, an accurately thrown pass and a well-timed leap and reception by the jumper, a perfectly executed alley-oop is a thing of beauty.

The take-it-to-the-hoop or flying slam dunk represents an even higher level of skill. Here, the player must move horizontally as well as vertically, and the shot must be taken off the dribble. (In a game, the player is allowed to take two steps between his last dribble and the takeoff for the shot.) This move calls for good acceleration and quick, instinctive body movements in addition to great leaping ability.

The last and most spectacular variety is the freestyle slam dunk. Here, the player is not required to dribble the ball or face a defender, so his performance is limited only by physical skill and imagination. A player can show off moves that he rarely gets to use in a game because they are too bizarre, too difficult, or just plain illegal. The best freestyle dunks involve an amazing array of windmills, double-pumps, 360s, tomahawks, and the sometimes unnameable.

HISTORY OF THE SLAM

The slam dunk was unknown in the early days of basketball. Many of the players of the 1940s and 1950s were quite capable of dunking the ball, but to do so was to invite retaliation, either by having your legs taken out from under you on the way down or by getting whacked later on the elbow or forearm when the

Wilt Chamberlain:
At 7-foot-1, Wilt Chamberlain's agility and unstoppable dunks put him in the Basketball Hall of Fame. He was active between 1959–1973.

referee wasn't looking. In those prehistoric days, a slam dunk was considered an insult that had to be answered.

The entrance of Wilt Chamberlain into the NBA in 1959 represented a key evolutionary turning point. At 7-foot-1, Wilt could dunk the ball easily, and it soon became his calling card. With his great physical strength and remarkable agility for a man of his size, Chamberlain was virtually unstoppable. Even the best defenders could only hope to deny him position under the hoop once in a while.

The slam dunk's rising popularity was due to the founding of a rival professional league, the American Basketball Association (ABA), in 1967. In an effort to attract fans, the new league emphasized a more wide-open, offensive game. The greatest star of the ABA was Julius Erving, who, with his huge hands, could hold a basketball as if it were a grapefruit. Whether in the open court or on a fast break or in the half-court against one or more defenders, Dr. J's graceful, soaring moves to the hoop redefined the standards of the slam dunk. Erving's signature move was his tomahawk dunk, in which he brandished the ball overhead—arm fully extended—as he approached the hoop. With the merger of the two leagues in 1976, Dr. J was able to bring his game to a nationwide audience.

Today, nearly every NBA player can slam-dunk, and the move has become almost commonplace. Virtually every team has one high-flying dunker. Names like Clyde "the Glide" Drexler of the Portland Trail Blazers and Karl "the Mailman" Malone of the Utah Jazz were among the marquee players known for their astonishing dunks. The list of great dunkers is a long one. However, it is generally recognized that to this day, only players of the caliber of Michael Jordan of the Chicago Bulls and Dominique Wilkins of the Atlanta Hawks have surpassed Erving in terms of spectacular mind-bending moves.

THE PHYSICALITY OF THE DUNK

What are the physical requirements needed to be able to dunk a basketball? The obvious requirement is, of course, that you have to be able to get the basketball over the edge of a ten-foot-high rim. This, in turn, calls for a combination of body height and jumping ability. It is also extremely helpful to be able to palm—grip securely with one hand—the ball. While it is not impossible to dunk the ball if you can't palm it, the variety and creativity of your dunks will be limited.

As a minimum requirement, you have to get your wrist to rim level in order to dunk the ball. This means that the sum of your standing reach and vertical leap must be 10 feet 6 inches or more. Your standing reach is essentially the distance from the floor to the tips of your fingers when you are reaching upward from a standing position. Using some basic observations about human anatomy, we can devise an approximate formula that relates vertical reach to body height. The length of a person's arm is about half the distance from his shoulder to the floor. If we take a person's body height in inches (H), subtract the distance from the top of the head to the shoulder (about 12 inches on average), and then add back half of this distance (about one arm's length), we arrive at the formula $R = 3(H-12)/2$, where R is the individual's standing reach in inches.

The difference between your vertical reach and 10 feet 6 inches—the minimum height that must be attained for a successful dunk—must be made up by jumping. For example, a 6-footer with a standing vertical reach of 7 feet 6 inches must have a vertical leap of at least 36 inches to get into dunking range.

What constitutes a good vertical leap? The average playground basketball player has a vertical leap of about 18 to 24 inches. Anything in the range of 24 to 36 inches is considered unusual, and any vertical leap over 36 inches is considered exceptional. The best vertical leap ever recorded for a basketball player is 48 inches, set by Darrell Griffith in 1976. In the history of the NBA, probably only a handful of players have had vertical leaps exceeding 42 inches. Most of the great acrobatic dunkers, like Jordan and Wilkins, were in the 36-to-40-inch range.

If you would like to know what your own vertical leap is, you can measure it fairly easily. Just stand facing a wall, extend your arm upward, and make a mark with a pencil or piece of chalk. This is your vertical reach. Now jump vertically as high as you can, making a second mark on the wall. The difference between the two marks is your vertical leap.

Given the size and athletic ability of any hoopster good enough to make it to the NBA, or even for that matter to any top-ranked Division I college team, we should not be overly impressed by anyone 6 feet 6 inches tall or more being able to dunk. All that's needed is a fairly ordinary leaping ability. It's far more impressive to see someone dunk a ball when he is 6 feet 3 inches and has a vertical leap of 30 to 33 inches.

Given this criterion, perhaps the most amazing dunker of recent years is not Jordan or Wilkins, but none other than Spud Webb of the Atlanta Hawks. Listed at 5 feet 7 inches tall, Webb had a vertical leap in the 42-to-45-inch range. Or consider David Thompson, who played for the Denver Nuggets in the 1970s and

Spud Webb:
It's not always how tall you are but how high you can jump that counts. Even though he is only 5-foot-7, Spud Webb of the Atlanta Hawks (active between 1985–1998) had a vertical leap of between 42 and 45 inches. Likewise, David Thompson stood 6-foot-4 as a player for the Denver Nuggets, but a vertical leap of 42 inches allowed him to extend a foot and a half above the rim.

1980s. Standing 6 feet 4 inches, with a vertical leap of 42 inches, Thompson was capable of lifting a basketball a foot and half above the rim.

To players and fans alike, the great slam dunkers appear to be airborne for seconds at a time and seem to hang in the air almost at will. In truth, their flight times are surprisingly short. According to the laws of physics, an athlete's hang time depends entirely on his upward speed at the moment of takeoff and cannot be extended once he is airborne.

In fact, hang time and vertical leap are mathematically related. The formula relating the vertical leap V (measured in inches) to the hang time (measured in seconds) is $V = 48$ squared. According to this equation, a vertical leap of 48 inches translates to a hang time of exactly one second. A 36-inch vertical leap corresponds to a hang time of 0.87 second. As unbelievable as it may seem, the great high flyers in the NBA perform their greatest moves in the space of eight- and nine-tenths of a second. No small part of Michael Jordan's greatness was the fact that he seemed to cover great distances in the air. He accentuated this illusion by releasing his shots on the way down, rather than at the peak of his trajectory.

WHY THE EXCITEMENT?

Clearly, it's not a big deal for almost any NBA player to dunk a basketball. So why are fans so excited by the sight of 7-foot players jamming one down? And why do players get so turned on by what for them is really not a difficult accomplishment?

It's easy to see why the fans are so impressed. After all, the act of dunking a basketball is far beyond the capability of the average spectator, who is as likely to dunk the ball as he is to set foot on the moon.

As for the players, they are all large, well-built individuals, capable of acts of great physical strength. Yet shooting a basketball almost always requires a soft touch, calling for a carefully modulated and rather gentle application of force rather than an explosion of brute strength.

Slam-dunking a basketball is perhaps the only opportunity a player ever gets to really unload in a game. To be able to break through the confines of a tight pressure defense, to get close enough to the basket with the ball in your hands, and to go up and over a tough defender and throw the ball down through the hoop with as much force as you please just plain feels good. When a great player unloads, it can be both intimidating and inspiring.

HIGH FLYER

Basic

Alley-oop

Flying

Freestyle

Michael Jordan of the Chicago Bulls and Washington Wizards is widely acknowledged as the game's premier slam dunker, as well as among the best players ever to play in the National Basketball Association. Jordan had an arsenal of dunks at his command. Yet they basically fell within four classifications. As seen in the accompanying photographs of Jordan (from left to right, top to bottom), there is the basic slam dunk from a standing position, the alley-oop dunk off a pass, the flying slam dunk after spinning through defenders, and the freestyle slam dunk.

The freestyle dunk is the most instinctive and creative of moves to the basket. Jordan himself didn't know what he was going to do until after his feet left the ground. Good elevation and the ability to shoot while on the way down contributed to Jordan's seeming ability to defy the laws of gravity.

While freestyle dunking is perhaps the most visually exciting, the powerful flying slam dunk is perhaps the most devastating since it signals a serious breakdown in the opposition's defense.

Bowling

STRIKE FORCE

by JOHN G. FALCIONI

IN SPORTS LIKE
PROFESSIONAL FOOTBALL,
SUCCESS COMES AS
A DIRECT RESULT OF
SIZE, STRENGTH, AND
SPEED. SHOULDER PADS
AND HELMETS PROVIDE
SAFEGUARDS AGAINST
INJURY, BUT IN TERMS OF
PHYSICAL ATTRIBUTES,
EQUIPMENT CANNOT
IMPROVE WHAT MOTHER
NATURE HAS BESTOWED.
IN BOWLING, WHERE
STRENGTH IS NOT
ESSENTIAL TO GOOD
PERFORMANCE, BUT
NEVERTHELESS PLAYS
AN IMPORTANT ROLE, A
SERIES OF EQUIPMENT
DEVELOPMENTS HAVE
LEVELED THE PLAYING
FIELD FOR KEGLERS OF
ALL SIZES.

◀ PBA bowling champ
Peter Weber, active
from 1980 to the
present, is a power
stroker, combining
the high backswing
of a cranker with the
smooth timing of a
stroker.

Today, the combination of a resin ball and the proper arm
swing can make a 110-pound bowler rattle the pins as hard as a
200-pounder. Moreover, the revolutionary developments behind
bowling's new wave of balls promise to free the sport from the
shackles of a reputation created by the likes of Ralph Kramden
and Archie Bunker. The sport has become so sophisticated that
knowledge of engineering and physics is likely to prove more
helpful in throwing strikes than doing curls with a dumbbell.

BOWLING-BALL UPGRADES

But in a sport big on tradition, where equipment upgrades such as
the use of polyester in addition to rubber in a ball took decades,
the sudden introduction of intricate core configurations for
bowling balls and new reactive materials for their outer shells
have been met with some criticism and a lot of confusion.

Many standout bowlers are critical of these balls (which are
often called "cheaters"), arguing that players of lesser ability
and striking power are now ranking among the top of the
Professional Bowlers Association (PBA) prize-money list.
This may be an overstatement, but it is true that even among
amateurs the new balls are having a staggering effect. The
American Bowling Congress (ABC) in Greendale, Wisconsin,
reported that the number of perfect games—occurring when a
player rolls twelve strikes in a row for a 300 score—soared to
a national high of 17,654 during the 1992–93 winter bowling
season, the first full season following the introduction of resin
balls, versus 14,889 the previous season.

Introduction of the resin balls has even forced the ABC,
which regulates the sport, to issue new guidelines that stymie
manufacturers from illegally manipulating specifications such as
a ball's coefficient of friction, coefficient of restitution, moment
of inertia, and radius of gyration.

Essentially, resin bowling balls provide the two most important
factors that increase the probability of striking: greater angle of
entry into the pocket and greater energy transfer. Polished, these
balls skid straight through the "heads," the oily first 45 feet of the
lane, and then snap strongly in the "back end," the last 15 feet.

Resin balls produce significantly lower friction than traditional high-friction urethane balls, especially on the oily part of the lane, says Daniel Speranza, a mechanical engineer and manager of the equipment-specifications department at the ABC. But on the drier end, near the pins, resin balls appear to have higher friction than regular urethane balls. This results in a greater angle of impact into what's known as the "pocket"—for right-handers, the area on a lane between the headpin and the No. 3 pin, or between the headpin and the No. 2 pin for left-handers. In general, a greater entry angle to the pocket produces more strikes.

What makes these balls react so drastically on dry lanes is a heavily guarded proprietary chemical recipe. Manufacturers say that resin balls are created the same way existing urethane balls are made, except that the resin additive is mixed in. Bowling-ball makers have aligned themselves with chemical suppliers who concoct resin formulations for different companies. For example, the giant chemical supplier BASF Corporation developed a product with the trade name Versathane for a ball called Nuke, designed by Texas-based Track Inc.

THE CORE SHAPE

What differentiates balls of similar cover stock is the shape of the inner core. Brunswick Corporation, one of the world's leading producers of bowling equipment and supplies, is recognized as having taken the first serious foray into the core of the ball to predict reaction and consistency, the hallmark of good bowling performance. With its Phantom family of urethane balls, introduced in late 1991, Brunswick showed how the size, shape, and location of the core in a ball chiefly determined its rotation and reaction as it travels through and across the oil pattern on a lane.

Knowing how a ball is supposed to react, if released correctly, is important because, like different greens on a golf course, bowling lanes vary greatly. In fact, the oil pattern of even a single lane will change several times during a game, causing the ball to react one way during the early frames and differently by the end of the game. The reason for this is the shifting of the oil used to condition the lanes. A mineral oil is applied to all lanes once a day to protect the wood from the pounding of the balls. Typically, the first 25 to 40 feet of a lane are oiled, with a heavy concentration applied to the middle of the lane and a medium concentration on the outside edges.

The number of balls rolled on a lane will change the lane conditions, and so will the temperature inside and outside the

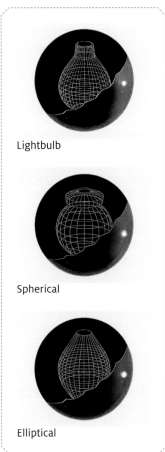

Lightbulb

Spherical

Elliptical

bowling center. Therefore, a lane condition will change even if no one is bowling on it because of the evaporation of the oil. That's why predicting how a ball will react is essential to consistency.

"The shape of the core is significant in predicting reaction because it provides the dynamic stability to maintain the preferred axis of rotation after drilling the grip holes," says Ray Edwards, an engineer and former professional bowler who became a research and development specialist at Brunswick.

Bowling balls are produced in two or three pieces depending upon the desired effect. Traditional three-piece balls provide a controlled and "true" roll. These balls feature a weight block of two to four ounces added to the core during manufacture. The block compensates for the weight that is removed by drilling the grip holes. Two-piece balls consist of a single-piece core and the cover stock. These balls generally begin to roll earlier on the lane than three-piece balls. Missouri-based manufacturer Faball Inc. is credited with developing the two-piece ball, now the favored construction method.

The cores themselves are made of a resin system and high- and low-density fillers. A good example of the new breed of bowling ball was a triple-density ball produced by Track Inc. called Critical Mass, which features a distinctive heavy ceramic circular core inside its regular lightbulb-shaped core. The ball is topped off with the same Versathane cover stock used in the company's Nuke ball.

"This ball is capable of generating the lowest radius of gyration possible to achieve maximum revolutions with less hand action," says Phil Cardinale, the former president of Track. The hard ceramic core of the ball was designed to begin rolling on the oily part of the lane, as a urethane ball does, and then, because of its resin shell, react sharply in the back end of the lane. By not skidding through the oil, this ball was designed to provide the advantage of a urethane roll with the power of a resin ball. (Radius of gyration measures how the mass and density of a ball are distributed. A ball with a higher radius of gyration will travel in a straight path for a longer period of time.)

Critical Mass was innovative because it was the first to use a heavy ceramic core. Meanwhile, Brunswick even started a new company called Quantum BTV (Brunswick Technology Venture) that quickly introduced three new balls. These Quantum balls, says Bill Wasserberger, an engineer in the R&D department, preserved the rotational dynamics of 15- and 16-pound balls in lighter weights (10, 12, and 14 pounds). Each ball, regardless of weight, is designed to have the same maximum and minimum radius of gyration for a standard roll. The company is doing this by varying the shape of the core of each ball, within the same family, depending upon its weight.

Generally, ball weight affects reaction on the lanes. If you roll a 16-pound ball and a 12-pound ball with identical core shapes on a lane, the 12-pound ball will "hook long" or go straighter longer and make its break to the pins later. The Quantum balls were designed to react or break the same way regardless of weight.

CRANKERS VERSUS STROKERS

When it comes to releasing the ball, there are as many styles as there are bowlers. But among professionals, there are two basic methods: the power swing or the traditional swing. Many pros stick closely to one or the other, while most amateurs mix and match.

Resin balls allow strokers, accurate bowlers who lack a powerful strike ball, to "blow out the rack" with the best of the crankers. Despite his 6-foot-2-inch frame, 1993's hottest bowler and top money winner, Walter Ray Williams, Jr., was considered a stroker. By using Ebonite's Crush/R resin ball for his first shot in most of the bowling tournaments that year, the 33-year-old transformed the reaction of his ball into that of a cranker's. He was able to strike consistently on light hits to the pocket that would have left pins standing were he using a non-resin ball.

For crankers, or big-hook bowlers, however, resin balls have not had a major impact on their scores. Take unlikely power bowler Chris Warren. His physique is reminiscent of a Charles Atlas "before"

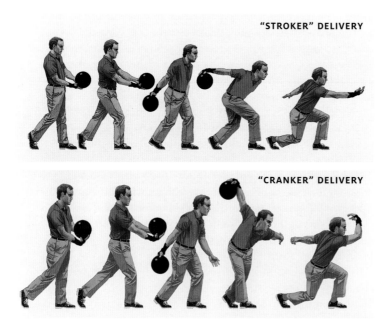

"STROKER" DELIVERY

"CRANKER" DELIVERY

The rendering shows a comparison between a right-handed "stroker" and a "cranker," each using a five-step approach. From left to right, the stroker (top) pushes the ball out in front of him in the second step, has a level backswing by the fourth step, and releases the ball smoothly during the sliding fifth step. To gain added leverage and power, the cranker (above) will open his right shoulder during the third step, as if to throw a roundhouse punch. By the fourth step, the ball will be above his shoulder and ready for a quick swing. At the point of release, the arm will snap up abruptly toward the head. The cranker's wrist will be cocked throughout the arm swing.

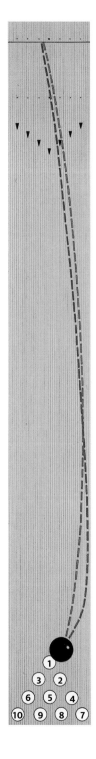

photo, yet the 5-foot-$4^1/_2$, 115-pound Texan throws the ball as hard as anyone on tour—118 mph.

Warren says he's always been a cranker. The keys to his success are foot speed and arm swing, which create momentum and leverage. Warren's foot speed, uncommon for many short players, allows him to raise his right arm quickly on the backswing. At the top of his swing, Warren opens his shoulder to gain the leverage necessary for a quick follow-through.

Additionally, power bowlers like Warren cup their wrist when releasing the ball so the ball rotates more, resulting in greater ball impact when it hits the pins. The final step occurs at the point of release, when a quick upward bend of the elbow produces what's known as lift on the ball. Lifting the ball complements cupping the ball in creating rotation.

Accuracy and consistency were keys to Brian Voss's success. Voss, winner of twenty-five PBA titles and more than $2.4 million in his professional career, is a cross between a cranker and a stroker. At 5-foot-10, his picture-perfect style generated the consistency to make him a perennial money winner. He too uses a resin ball.

"You cannot not use a resin ball these days. I'd be losing ten pins per game if I didn't use them," Voss says, "and that's too much when you have guys hitting the pocket with these balls."

For better or worse, resin balls have changed the game for good. In 1992, resin balls were perceived as a fad, but now they have become a mainstay, says Jim Mailander, president of the Maryland-based ball manufacturer Champions Bowling Products Corporation. "People thought the resin-ball popularity would die. If that's true, it's been one of the longest wakes in history."

◀ **Resin-Ball Track:**
Because a resin ball (red line) will skid through the "heads" of the lane and hook sharply into the pocket, the ball is released farther inside on the lane. Thus, when the ball begins hooking to the "pocket," the angle of impact will be greater that that of a non-resin ball (blue line).

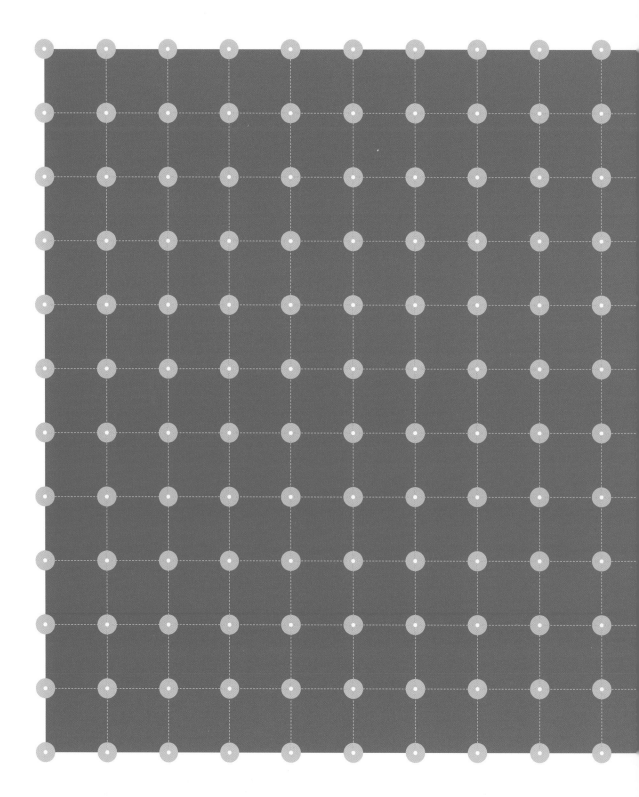

Boxing

THE KNOCKOUT PUNCH

by WILLIAM J. HOCHSWENDER

EVER SINCE THE ROMANS SUCCEEDED THE GREEKS AND CHANGED BOXING FROM AN HONORED MILITARY DISCIPLINE INTO A BLOOD SPECTACLE FOR THE ELITE, THE KNOCKOUT HAS BEEN THE GOAL OF THE SPORT. IT IS ONE OF THE FEW OCCASIONS IN ANY ATHLETIC CONTEST WHERE SYMBOLIC CONQUEST AND REAL CONQUEST MERGE. IT IS A KIND OF DEATH THAT RARELY BECOMES REAL.

◀ Mike Tyson, a famous practitioner of the knockout punch, plying his trade on the jaw of fellow heavyweight Larry Holmes during the fourth round of the World Heavyweight Championship in 1988.

It can be sudden and categorical—10 seconds in dreamland for the loser, absolute victory for the winner.

It can also be disturbing.

One thinks of Mike Tyson's 1986 first-round onslaught against Marvis Frazier, in which a rapid-fire sequence of uppercuts had Frazier's senseless head jerking and bobbing eerily atop his powerful frame. Or the 1988 Tyson–Larry Holmes finale, where the once dominant former champion was smashed into a dazed state before succumbing to a punch that snapped his head back violently and sent him flopping to the canvas like a lifeless doll.

Both of these climaxes illustrate important biomechanical and medical points about the nature of the knockout itself— how a fighter loses consciousness, why some boxers are bigger punchers than others, what constitutes a glass jaw, and so on. However, even when it comes to the brute force of the boxing ring, a knockout punch is so subtle and complex that it not only eludes our senses but baffles the understanding of scientists. The so-called sweet science still holds its mysteries.

THE MYSTERY OF BOXING

Certainly boxing, like most other sports, can be appreciated on many levels. The first-time observer at ringside will see and appreciate a much different prizefight than a veteran fan, or even an ex-boxer or trainer. Boxing insiders convincingly offer bits of wisdom that challenge the most educated conclusions of physicians.

Ray Arcel, who trained twenty world champions, from Barney Ross and Tony Zale to Roberto Duran and Larry Holmes, believes the knockout will always defy analysis. "I've seen guys go down from a light tap and not move," he says. "Of course, generally, there has to be some power behind the blow, but it's not how hard you get hit, but where and when you get hit. I don't think anybody can ever explain that."

Arcel cites the example of Jim Braddock, whom he trained to defend his heavyweight title against Joe Louis in 1937. "Braddock went out in the first round and hit Louis on the chin and put him on his back. No one could believe it because he wasn't a puncher. But he could take it. He had been hit harder by guys with more power and he'd survived. But then when Louis hit him, he went down."

Arcel also recalls a strange episode in the career of Ezzard Charles. In the 1940s and 1950s, Charles was a great boxer as a heavyweight champion, and no one could knock him out—not even Rocky Marciano, who fought him to a bloody decision. But in the last round of one of Charles's four fights with Jersey Joe Walcott, he got hit with a punch, Arcel remembers, "that could've knocked a wall down. Charles lasted out the round, but the punch, a left hook, left an impression."

The next time the two fighters met, the unstoppable Charles was stopped in the seventh round, flattened by a punch that came out of nowhere and which, Arcel believes, was a carbon copy of the punch he had earlier survived. "He just knew somewhere in his mind that it should have knocked him out."

BEHIND THE KNOCKOUT PUNCH

Technically, a knockout punch is simply a form of cerebral concussion. It results in either unconsciousness or a groggy state that makes it impossible for the boxer to rise from the canvas or continue. According to Dr. King Liu, a sports-medicine researcher formerly of the University of Iowa Medical School, "A concussion can be defined as a dramatic loss of consciousness caused by a disruption of the neurons in the reticular formation in the brain stem."

This means that when a blow is delivered to the head, it causes a variation—what Liu calls a high-pressure gradient—between the brain and the spinal cord, a twisting and tearing of the regulatory cells (neurons) that results in a shutdown. In other words, the jawbone sends a message to the brain: go to sleep.

Barry D. Jordan, medical director of the New York State Athletic Commission, divided the knockout into four categories of severity. In Type I, the boxer is dazed and unable to defend himself—out on his feet. This commonly results in a technical knockout. Type 2 is when the boxer is knocked to the canvas and cannot rise before the count of ten, yet remains conscious. In Type 3, the fighter is knocked unconsciousness but recovers quickly. Type 4 involves a longer period of unconsciousness.

CAUSE OF THE KO

Jordan, who published original research on the neurological aspects of boxing, is a student of the knockout. "Basically, what causes the KO is a rotational acceleration, a spinning of the brain," he says. "Picture the brain as, say, a mushroom or a cauliflower.

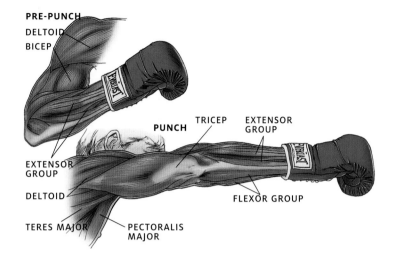

PRE-PUNCH
DELTOID
BICEP
TRICEP
PUNCH
EXTENSOR
GROUP
EXTENSOR
GROUP
DELTOID
FLEXOR GROUP
TERES MAJOR
PECTORALIS
MAJOR

A knockout punch can begin at the feet, ripple through the torso and culminate with a complex interaction of several muscle groups in the arm.

During a knockout, the stalk doesn't move, but the spin at the top causes you to lose consciousness. That's why headgear won't prevent KOs. It doesn't preclude the acceleration."

Professional boxers can deliver blows with such force to the movable head that the brain smacks against the skull, tearing nerve fibers, the meningeal sac that supports the brain and blood vessels. The direction and power of the blow determine the severity of this tearing.

There are two basic kinds of acceleration: rotational (or angular) and linear (or translational). The former tends to be caused by roundhouse punches or hooks, the latter by straight shots. According to Dr. Jordan, linear acceleration, caused by a punch that sends the head straight back, is not as likely to cause a KO. But, as he points out, "Obviously, the right amount of force can cause a KO: it depends upon where it is applied."

Referring to the Tyson-Holmes bout, Jordan observes that the first knockdown, a right to Holmes's temple—an example of linear movement—did cause acceleration. It left the former champ rubber-legged and uncoordinated—a Type I state.

A groggy fighter who has lost control of his neck muscles, as Holmes had, becomes even more vulnerable to sudden rotational acceleration. Thus, the final punch—maybe not as powerful as the first—a sweeping left uppercut to the point of the chin, rapidly swiveled Holmes's head, resulting in a Type 3 knockout. It's important to note that the severity of the punch in the Tyson-Holmes fight example is not the issue. The punch that flattened Holmes was hardly the kind of haymaker one associates with a knockout. The video replay indicated a lightning-quick poke to

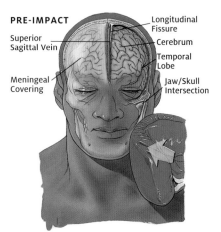

PRE-IMPACT

Superior Sagittal Vein

Meningeal Covering

Longitudinal Fissure

Cerebrum

Temporal Lobe

Jaw/Skull Intersection

The brain, meninges, and attendant blood vessels reside within the protective shell of the skull.

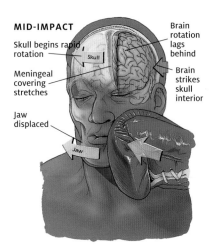

MID-IMPACT

Skull begins rapid rotation

Meningeal covering stretches

Jaw displaced

Brain rotation lags behind

Brain strikes skull interior

A blow to the head begins a rapid rotation of the skull, bruising the brain and meningeal covering.

the chin, followed by Holmes's head snapping, and a somewhat graceless collapse to the mat—reminiscent of a falling tree.

Here, it is worth mentioning that even a straight punch causes some degree of rotational acceleration. As Dr. Jordan has written, "In reality, the distinction between a punch that causes a purely rotational or linear acceleration is mostly theoretical, because the force produced by the blow is usually some variable combination of linear and rotational acceleration."

The linear component and the rotational component—individually or in concert—are the root cause of the knockout. And when these two dynamic boxing elements merge and mix, the mystery of the knockout only deepens.

OTHER KO FACTORS

There is one last type of acceleration, or rather deceleration, to be considered. This is not caused by punches but by the impact of the fighter's head on the canvas. The collision between the brain and the skull on rapid deceleration only aggravates the effects of rotation of the brain within the skull, and can lead to bruises on the brain's lobes.

Knockouts have also been known to result from injuries to the carotid, the chief artery passing up the neck to the brain—usually from a very powerful blow to the neck, which compresses the carotid sinus, deprives the brain of oxygen-carrying blood, and causes shock and injury to the cerebrum.

And then there are body punches. As Arcel observes, "I've seen boxers who could absorb a terrific amount of punishment get tapped in the solar plexus and go facedown."

PUNCHING POWER

So what makes a Louis or a Tyson so devastating a puncher? Moreover, what makes a physically unimposing boxer a knockout artist? And what makes one fighter better able to withstand a big blow than the next guy? Is there such a thing as a glass jaw?

As is well known to anyone who's had his fair share of fights, there are guys built like Arnold Schwarzenegger who couldn't KO a dandelion, and there are scrawny dudes who can flatten a truck with one shot. The mystery of punching power is elusive.

As Jackie Graham, former deputy commissioner of the New York State Athletic Commission, points out, George Foreman and Gerry Cooney are both known as arm punchers, fighters who don't maximize the force of the blow by using their bodies for leverage. Yet both somehow succeeded in knocking out most of their opponents—and quickly. Foreman and Cooney belie the

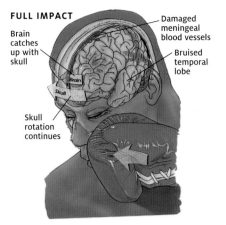

FULL IMPACT

Brain catches up with skull

Damaged meningeal blood vessels

Bruised temporal lobe

Brain

Skull

Skull rotation continues

▲ Rotation of the brain relative to the brain stem and the collision of the brain with the skull result in a knockout.

notion that punching power must be truly forceful to achieve a knockout. While a Joe Frazier or a Mike Tyson can accomplish knockouts by planting their feet and rotating their entire bodies behind the force of a blow, arm punchers seem to knock out their opponents with feathery quickness.

Graham remembers Lew Jenkins, a great lightweight champion of the 1930s: "He had hands the size of a little girl's and pipestem arms, and he was drunk half the time. Yet he could punch like a mule. It has to do with accuracy, direction, leverage, and who knows what else. As for durability, take my brother, Billy Graham. He fought 120 fights—and he was in with Sugar Ray Robinson, Carmen Basilio, Joey Giardello—and he was never even knocked down!"

POWER PRINCIPLES

Nevertheless, certain classic principles apply. As Dr. Jordan has written in the *Archives of Neurology*: "The concussive properties of a boxer's punch relate to the manner in which the punch is delivered and how the mechanical forces are transferred and absorbed through the intercranial cavity . . . The force transmitted by a punch is directly proportional to the mass of the glove and the velocity of the swing, and is inversely proportional to the total mass opposing the punch."

In essence, these are Newton's second and third laws. At the most basic level, the force of the punch is computed by size or mass of the gloved fist times its speed (force = mass X acceleration). But since we are discussing two bodies in motion, we must also consider that the force of the glove on the head is equal and opposite to the force of the head on the glove. This resistance of the head and neck to the effect of rotation must be considered when calculating the ability of a boxer to take a punch.

Newton's third law comes into play most intriguingly in the technique known as rolling with the punch. Many clever boxers, notably Muhammad Ali, diminish the impact of the blow by abruptly pulling back their head at the instant of collision—rolling with it, so to speak. In this manner, skull and brain accelerate more in unison, thus diffusing the damage of the blow.

It is easy to see, therefore, that a sudden, unexpected punch that catches a fighter unprepared, his jaw hung like a lantern, can result in a tremendous acceleration of the head. The soft brain, which does not move as fast as the skull itself, is deformed, with resultant stress to, and even tearing of, nerves and blood vessels in the brain's protective meninges.

An additional biomechanical factor is the duration of contact.

According to Dr. Liu, "Relatively low-magnitude blows with a long contact period can do the same job as a more forceful punch. A good analogy is found in karate. In trying to break a stack of bricks with a blow of your hand, you might discover that in the split second the force applied reaches a certain level and the pain in your hand is intense, you would withdraw, but a karate master maintains contact until the bricks are broken. A good boxer, in the same sense, follows through."

As to why some fighters can absorb more punishment than others, says Dr. Liu, "Individual variations in the way brains are constructed enable some people to sustain a higher brain pressure gradient—or rotational acceleration—than others. It's simply part of the variation in all of nature."

Do some boxers suffer from the so-called "glass jaw"? Ray Arcel contends that the term is nothing more than "a newspaper expression."

"We never used it," Arcel explains. "Certain areas, certain nerve centers, in some individuals, may be more susceptible to a punch. In my own experience, certain guys were made of sterner stuff than others. Let's face it. The human body was never made to be punched."

True. But since the advent of this primordial sport, the human body has absorbed and delivered countless blows. Perfecting the knockout punch has been and always will be the ultimate goal in a competition mixing skill and toughness with what professional boxers know as an inner, indefinable fire.

THE SCIENCE OF A BOXING KNOCKOUT

by MARITA VERA

This article was published in
POPULAR MECHANICS in 2010.

BOXING FANS LIVE FOR THE THRILL OF A KNOCKOUT PUNCH. BUT THAT KO COMES AT A STEEP PHYSICAL PRICE FOR THE VICTIM. RIGHT JAB, LEFT HOOK, RIGHT JAB, AND THEN . . . BAM! KNOCKOUT. THERE IS NOTHING MORE EXHILARATING FOR A BOXING AUDIENCE THAN TO SEE A FIGHTER HIT THE MAT IN A KNOCKOUT. BUT BEING ON THE LOSING END OF A KO PUNCH CAN DAMAGE A LOT MORE THAN A PUGILIST'S PRIDE— RESEARCH SUGGESTS THAT THE BLOWS THAT CAUSE KNOCKOUTS CAN BE DEBILITATING TO A BOXER'S SHORT- AND LONG-TERM HEALTH.

◀ This dramatic knockout by Manny Pacquiao occured in the sixth round in his highly publicized 2012 match against Juan Manuel Márquez IV.

So what causes a knockout? Concussions, and lots of them. While it often seems as though the effect is caused by a single well-placed shot, it is usually the result of many quick punches. Each punch creates a concussion (technically defined as any head injury that causes a disruption of neurological function), and each concussion brings the boxer closer to a state of darkness.

Here's how it happens: The body contains dissolved sodium, potassium and calcium, collectively known as electrolytes, which are responsible for conducting impulses along neurons. Every time a fighter receives a blow to a nerve, potassium leaves the cell and calcium rushes in, destabilizing the electrolyte balance, while the brain does all it can to keep these levels in balance. With each successive blow, this balance becomes harder and harder to maintain, and more and more energy must be spent in the process. When the body reaches the point where the damage outweighs the body's ability to repair itself, the brain shuts down to conserve enough energy to fix the injured neurons at a later point.

"After a brain injury, the heart must supply sufficient blood flow for the brain to repair itself. If the demand outweighs the supply the brain then shuts down and leads to an eventual loss of consciousness," says Anthony Alessi, M.D., a neurologist and ringside physician for the Connecticut State Boxing Commission. "That's when I know to end the match, because if we keep going the fighter is going to die."

Surprisingly, the boxer's feet are often the first clear signal that he is on the verge of being knocked out. When the neural networks that emanate from the cerebellum (the part of the brain responsible for coordinating motor activity) are disrupted by a concussion, a fighter loses his ability to coordinate foot movements.

"They become flat-footed, which is the inability to adjust. Boxers can't move forward or backward quickly," Alessi says. "As you watch their feet, you realize that the same lack of coordination is going on in their upper extremities in their hands. And eventually they are unable to defend themselves."

Once their feet start to go, they are often just a single punch away from a knockout.

Lacrosse

APPROACH
AND TAKEOFF

LACROSSE IS WAR. OR, AT LEAST, WAR'S YOUNGER SIBLING. FIRST PLAYED BY THE NATIVE NORTH AMERICANS, THE SPORT HAS BEEN KNOWN AS *BAGGATAWAY* AND "THE LITTLE BROTHER OF WAR" BY ITS CRE-ATORS AND WAS PRACTICED AS BOTH A PREPARATION FOR BATTLE AS WELL AS AN ALTERNATIVE TO IT BY WHICH MINOR DISAGREEMENTS BETWEEN NEIGHBOR-ING SETTLEMENTS WERE RESOLVED.

The modern game redefines the parameters of play from a village-wide event contested over multiple days to dimensions and duration resembling other field sports like football and rugby.

The movement and strategies of possession are similar to basketball and soccer, as a well-spaced offense runs and passes the ball in a procession down the field that is met physically by defenders who may check body or stick to disrupt the incursion into their territory. Ultimately, a shot will be set up and the game decided by an explosion of rotational momentum applied to 5.5 ounces of hard Indian rubber that must be stopped or redirected in less than two-tenths of a second.

JIM BROWN: ALL AMERICAN

It was said of Jim Brown, who ranks among the legends of the NFL and left the game as the all-time leading rusher (still ranked in the top-10), that football was his second-best sport. Brown, who was also a decathlon athlete, a varsity basketball player,

▶ Jim Brown, a legend of Lacrosse, at Syracuse. He was included into the Lacrosse Hall of Fame in 1983, and was named a first-team All-American in lacrosse in 1955 (pictured).

a boxer, and a standout pitcher having thrown two no-hitters in high school, was considered by many to be the greatest lacrosse player of all time. Brown possessed a blistering underhand shot, discouraged by most modern coaches as it tends to be less accurate than other styles, but clearly not a problem for the All-American lacrosse star who scored 43 goals in 10 games to lead Syracuse University to an undefeated season during his senior year while finishing second for the national scoring title. It was his dominance that led to a rule-change requiring those in possession of the ball to keep the stick in constant motion.

John Brenkus of ESPN's Sport Science looked back on Brown's career and determined that at top speed he could create "an estimated 1,000 pounds of force with each powerful stride" while his lacrosse shots were "generated with roughly 4,000 watts of peak power." This translates into an athlete with great acceleration (force = mass x acceleration) and the ability to expend near-superhuman levels of energy in quick bursts (power = energy/time). If you were building the perfect lacrosse player it is these two traits that you'd start with, as we'll see when we look closer at the physics and fundamentals behind a powerful shot.

THE POWER OF PAUL RABIL

Jim Brown was a once-in-a-generation caliber athlete, who controlled the game through speed, ferocity, and ingenuity. As a part-owner of the Major League Lacrosse's New York Lizards, Brown has reunited with the sport he played purely for the love of it, and has been introduced to the modern professional game from the owner's box. If there's one element of today's game consistent with Brown's playing days, it's power. In professional lacrosse, whether it be the MLL or the indoor National Lacrosse League, the one name most synonymous with power is Paul Rabil.

Paul Rabil follows through on his shot at The Fastest Shot Competition during the 2010 Major League Lacrosse All-Star Game on July 8, 2010 at Harvard Stadium in Boston, Massachusetts.

Paul Rabil may be the first breakout star of professional lacrosse, with a range of corporate sponsors that include Red Bull, Polk Audio, and New Balance among others. A three-time MLL Offensive Player of the year, league MVP, and integral part of the Boston Cannons 2011 MLL Championship season, Rabil has also taken home Division 1 and World Championships as well as the NLL's Championship Cup while playing with the Washington Stealth. The driving force behind Rabil's championship resume is the surge of power he unleashes when he attacks the goal, perfectly displayed in the 111 mile-per-hour world record shot he recorded at the 2009 MLL All-Star Game, repeated for good measure the following year.

Rabil's record (now shared with Kyle Hartzell, who hit the mark at the 2012 All-Star Game) is about 10 miles an hour above his average in-game shot. By comparison, when a baseball player steps to the plate to face a 90 mile per hour pitcher he has .44 hundredths of a second to react. That would translate to .39 hundredths of a second for a lacrosse goalie if the shot were coming from sixty feet and six inches away, like it does on the baseball diamond. The typical lacrosse shot can come from ten yards out or less, giving the man in the cage .19 to stop a bullet.

LINEAR MOMENTUM

Elite lacrosse players like Brown and Rabil share in their ability to fire off a shot with explosive results. More often than not the fuse for each was directly sparked by their blazing speed. Using a basic equation to illustrate, linear momentum (p) is the product of mass (m) and velocity (v); the momentum of the player himself, created by his weight and speed as he approaches the goal (p=mv), can be a catalyst in the transformation of a lacrosse ball into an almost unstoppable projectile. The most dangerous shooters in the game can harness their speed and transfer it from the vector in which they are travelling into the rotation that defines their shot, employing a shooting technique that will allow them to achieve maximum efficiency.

>>>

ROTATIONAL MOMENTUM

Not every shot requires a runaway train to propel it. Linear momentum can be generated in a single powerful step, much like a baseball player stepping into his swing prior to launching a moonshot over the centerfield bleachers. The friction generated as the shooter drives his foot into the turf is where linear momentum begins its conversion to rotational momentum, as the shooter transfers energy from his planted foot through his legs and hips, up the torso and into his shoulders—which will become the axis of rotation from which even greater speed can be applied to the ball before it is fired.

As the stick head with the ball pocketed inside rotates around the player's body it picks up the speed it needs to become an effective shot. The linear speed of an object is directly proportional to its distance from the axis of rotation; the further away it is from the center, the greater the speed at which it moves. Think of two horses on a merry-go-round, both set even to each other as they travel around the carousel. If you drew the path of each horse you'd have a larger circle for the outside horse, and from that you'd conclude that in creating the larger circle the outer horse had to travel a greater distance, and to go further than its companion while maintaining an equal position it must have also travelled at a greater speed.

When the object in question is a lacrosse ball poised to scream through the air as if it were fired from a cannon, both arm movement and stick length determine the distance it travels around the shooter's body. As Paul Rabil comes bearing down on a goalie, he can extend the head of his 40-inch lacrosse stick an additional 22 inches away from him in the course of a well-executed shot. With the ball in motion over five feet away from his shoulders, Rabil's rotational momentum at the point of release has been measured at 1,350 degrees per second.

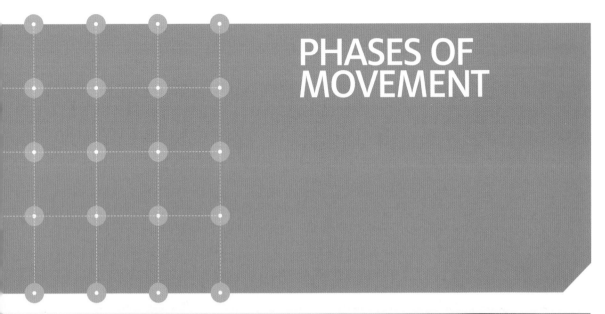

PHASES OF MOVEMENT

CARL RUNK WON A NATIONAL CHAMPIONSHIP COACHING LACROSSE AT TOWSON UNIVERSITY IN 1974 AND SAW THE PROGRAM TAKE ITS PLACE AMONG THE NATION'S BEST WITH MULTIPLE NCAA DIVISION I TOURNAMENT APPEARANCES OVER THE NEXT TWO DECADES, INCLUDING A TRIP TO THE CHAMPIONSHIP GAME IN 1991.

Coach Runk stepped down as Towson head coach after the 1998 season, but remained in the kinesiology department and later began coaching at the high school level, leading his squads to Maryland State Championships in 2003 and 2008.

When asked about the physical attributes he prioritized while recruiting, it should come as no surprise that outside of the coordination required to handle the stick Coach Runk's top two most valued traits in a prospective player were both driving elements in the creation of force and momentum—quickness and size. Of course, recruitment is only the collection of raw players that still need to be developed, and as much as physics can explain where the power comes from in a well-shot ball and why it travels as fast as it does, proper shooting technique is necessary to put a player in position to take advantage of the forces around him. Coach Runk detailed the three phases of movement that he teaches to his new players before every season as part of his discussion on shooting.

PREPARATION PHASE

According to Coach Runk, the preparation phase determines "the position of the stick just before the forward movement." As the attacker makes his approach he must ensure that the stick is in the ready so that the ball may travel a great enough distance along its arc to generate power prior to the shot. Runk explains the positioning not with a specific placement and location of hands and equipment (although both will factor depending on the situation), but with the understanding that preparation for the next phase (power) means being in position to execute a 90 degree stick movement, the end of which will be aligned with the target. "It is the preparation phase that determines the length of the 'power phase' that follows," says Runk. As part of the preparation for the shot, a player might crank the stick back to give the head a greater distance to travel and generate speed from.

Once the shooter plants his foot and commits to the shot, his mechanics will take over, and if he does so out of position with insufficient distance between the top of the arc and his intended release point "he will not reach full potential when shooting the

ball." In essence, the preparation phase determines how much potential energy before the shot will be available for transfer to kinetic energy during it.

POWER PHASE

The power phase determines the magnitude of force applied in creating velocity as upper body torque and quickness are used to generate linear speed. As Coach Runk describes it "an example of the complete 'power phase' movement would be a player standing at the 15 or 20 yard line, in front of the cage, with his shoulders facing the sideline. The head of the stick would be positioned toward the midfield line ('Point A'). The power phase is initiated from 'Point A' to its conclusion at 'Point B,' when the stick head is facing the sidelines and the ball is released—a distance of approximately 90 degrees. The quickness in acceleration of the stick head from 'Point A' to 'Point B' will determine the velocity of the shot."

This phase employs the rotational elements that contribute to momentum, and each one represents a variable that will influence the velocity of the shot. Shorter distances and a lack of speed will result in a weaker shot, and conversely, creating a larger arc and maintaining quickness and speed will generate greater velocity.

FOLLOW THROUGH

This is the final phase of the shooting technique, and its objective is to "create a movement directed towards total efficiency." A proper follow through extends the movement of the shot in a unified manner, decelerating the body toward recovery. Coach Runk believes that "any altering in the follow-through phase has a tendency to affect total potential."

SHOOTING STYLES

There are five shooting styles common to the game: the over-the-shoulder or three-quarter-arm shot, the sidearm shot, the underhand shot, the one-hand shot, and the backhand shot. Each shot is a tool in the lacrosse player's belt, allowing him to present the defense with different looks as well as create an alternate arc path of greater distance to ultimately generate more velocity.

[1] **THE OVER-THE-SHOULDER OR THREE-QUARTER-ARM SHOT:** According to Bob Scott, hall-of-fame lacrosse coach from Johns Hopkins University, the over-the-shoulder shot is "the most effective of all the shots because it gives the greatest accuracy," which is "the most important factor in shooting" by Scott's standards.

Scott believed the precision of the over-the-shoulder shot did not rob it of its explosiveness, stating "it has as much power behind it as the other shots." As the name implies, the shot is taken with the upper hand over the shooter's shoulder before power is applied by way of a snap of the wrist in concert with the violent pull of the stick's butt end from the lower hand and a shift in body weight from rear

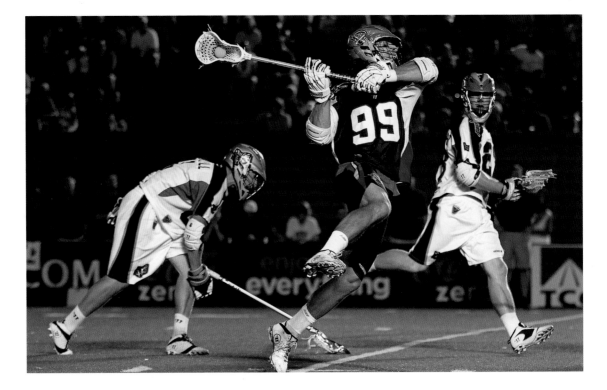

to front leg. The whole motion resembles that of a baseball player firing in the ball from the outfield with the bottom hand acting as a fulcrum. A well-executed over-the-shoulder shot the head of the stick will see the stick take a 180-degree path, releasing at the halfway mark and pointing toward the floor at its conclusion.

[2] **THE SIDEARM SHOT:** Kyle Wharton's devastating sidearm shot brought him YouTube fame when he deployed it while playing for Johns Hopkins against Towson, the impact tearing clean through the back of the net and leaving a hole big enough for hundreds of thousands of YouTube views to pour in through. The sidearm shot employs an almost identical technique as the three-quarter, but when shooting sidearm the head of the stick will travel along a path below the shoulder. Coach Scott discussed the merits of the shot, noting that "if the head of the stick goes no lower than the shooter's belt, the sidearm shot can be developed to a point where it is effective from a stationary or slow-moving position." Scott believes the shot should be avoided while on the run, as it is harder to control than it's over-the-shoulder counterpart.

[3] **THE UNDERHAND SHOT:** Jim Brown's preferred shot, the underhand

shot is similar to the over-the-shoulder and sidearm but the path of the stick head now travels below the knees, making it most difficult to control. Coach Scott believed that unless a player could keep an underhand shot on target for three of every four shots he took, he should discard it from his repertoire. By Scott's account, in twenty years of coaching "only three or four players [were] given the green light to shoot the underhand shot."

[4] **THE ONE-HAND SHOT:** Typically a close-range shot powered by the snap of the wrist on top of a one-handed sidearm or underhand motion, the one-hand shot is best for catching defensemen off guard. The power generated tends to be limited, making the shot most effective from within five yards of the crease. It should be no surprise that the exception to this rule was Jim Brown, who once scored on a 16-yard one-hander during the 1957 North-South College All-Star game.

[5] **THE BACKHAND SHOT:** A close-range shot whose stick path mirrors all of the previous shots, the backhand shot can surprise a defender by providing an unexpected trajectory. When capably wielded it can also give the attacker an interference-free response to a defenseman who has used his stick to block the forehand.

Football

THE MECHANICS OF THE BOMB

by JOHN BAKKE

FOOTBALL MAY BE A GAME OF INCHES, BUT A LONG PASS—THE BOMB—TAKES THEM BY THE THOUSANDS, BREAKING THE SPORT'S GROUND-ATTACK PATTERN IN A SINGLE LONG-DISTANCE GAMBIT. IT'S FOOTBALL'S SLAM DUNK, ITS HOME RUN. NOTHING ELSE CAN ACCOMPLISH SO MUCH SO QUICKLY OR WITH SO MUCH EXCITEMENT.

◀ Quarterback Andrew Luck of the Indianapolis Colts was the No. 1 draft selection in the 2012 NFL Draft.

Part of the play's drama is its all-or-nothing style, but those who know best insist the bomb is more craft than crapshoot. Indeed, its success relies on timing and coordination from the players, as well as smooth and accurate lofting of a ball not particularly suited to easy flight.

INTRICACIES OF THE PLAY

For the football strategist, precise timing is the key. "It's far more important than arm strength," says Don Shula, the Hall of Fame coach who led the National Football League's (NFL) Miami Dolphins to a perfect season in 1972 and amassed 347 wins between 1963 and 1996.

The play's development actually can be faster than passing plays, covering less distance. With the need for quickness, the quarterback customarily drops back only five steps, instead of the usual seven. In that time—just three to four seconds—the receiver has moved downfield ten or fifteen yards and is just coming alongside the player defending him.

This is a crucial moment in the play, in two regards.

First, the receiver must be positioned to move past his defender and stay ahead of him the rest of the way. If he isn't, the critical timing is destroyed. If he is, the rest of the play is an all-out sprint for another 30 to 35 yards to where, if all goes well, the ball will be waiting for him.

Second, the pass itself must be launched to near perfection, possibly with defenders closing in. The quarterback must throw to a spot some 50 yards away, where the intended receiver will not be for another four to five seconds. The margin of error may be only one yard in either direction.

Quarterback Dan Marino is one reason why Shula's Dolphins led the NFL in 1987–88 with an average of nearly 260 passing yards per game.

"Like any passing pattern, timing is essential," says Marino, whose NFL records for most career touchdown passes (420), most career yards (61,361), and most career passes completed (4,967) stood unchallenged for many years, before being surprised by Brett Favre.

As delicate a feat as it seems on the field, throwing an accurate bomb is even more remarkable when considered in a mechanical context. Spin, angle of attack, trajectory, and velocity all combine to bring a football into the hands of its intended receiver.

PRINCIPLES OF PIGSKIN AERODYNAMICS

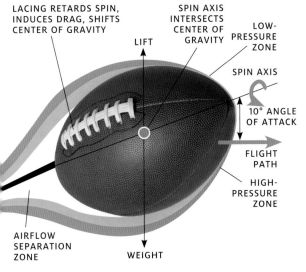

LACING RETARDS SPIN, INDUCES DRAG, SHIFTS CENTER OF GRAVITY

LIFT

SPIN AXIS INTERSECTS CENTER OF GRAVITY

LOW-PRESSURE ZONE

SPIN AXIS

10° ANGLE OF ATTACK

FLIGHT PATH

HIGH-PRESSURE ZONE

AIRFLOW SEPARATION ZONE

WEIGHT

⏭ A spin-stabilized airborne football has reduced drag because of its elliptical shape. Extra-long yardage is gained when low-pressure airflow passing over the top of the football produces lift, just like an airplane wing. A perfect pass results when a football's spin axis maintains a 10-degree angle of attack relative to trajectory along its entire flight path.

THE BALL

The most significant consideration in a football's flight is also the most obvious—its shape. A football can present many different profiles to the air it sails through, with the forces governing its flight varying considerably.

"Aerodynamically, a football is a very unstable object," says Professor Pasquale Sforza, head of the aerospace engineering department at Polytechnic University of New York. "Baseballs and other spheres are very stable by comparison."

The fundamental effect of its oblong shape is a lack of stability, with a resulting need for spin, which creates a steadying gyroscopic effect.

To throw a good spiral, the quarterback must spin the ball around an axis that runs lengthwise through the center of the ball. If the spin axis is off, the pass will assume a drag-inducing wobble.

Assuming perfect spin, a football's angle of attack can still vary—that is, the position of its nose in relation to the trajectory, which is the same as the path traveled by the ball's center of gravity.

If the ball is at a positive angle of attack, with the nose above the direction of flight, air forcing its way over and under the ball will give it some lift, much like an airplane wing.

When air passes over any object, there is always some drag. For a football, the coefficient of drag can vary. From studies of a rotating projectile in axial flow (spinning the same way a football does), one might conclude that the drag coefficient would decrease with the speed of the spiral. Unfortunately for the quarterback, though, the spin would likely have to be well over 1,000 rpm, whereas the typical good pass is in the range of 600 rpm.

Angles of Attack: Drag decreases with longer projectiles—like bullets and spinning footballs.

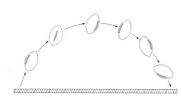

Pass Interference: The angle of the spin axis relative to trajectory widens in the later stages of flight, causing the ball to tumble.

Path to Completion: A true bomb maintains its 10-degree angle of attack for the entire length of the quarterback's intended flight path.

VELOCITY

Velocity is a different story. The faster the ball travels, the lower the coefficient of drag. Curiously, for a sphere there is one range where the drag coefficient drops considerably with only a slight increase in velocity, so throwing just a touch harder will mean far less deceleration due to drag. For a football, there is no data to support a similar effect. But aerodynamicists think it might occur in the range of 40 to 45 mph.

Here too, the gyroscopic phenomenon brought about by the spin comes into play. Beyond basic stabilization, this effect maintains and self-corrects the ball's orientation. Consider a rising pass, the ball's nose pointed upward and its spin axis aligned ideally with the trajectory. As the ball ascends, reaches its apex, and starts to descend, the nose slowly continues to tip forward and ultimately points downward because—in the same way that a gyroscope resists disruption, or a top returns to its upright position when slightly disturbed—the football's spin acts to keep the spin axis and trajectory aligned, maintaining maximum lift and minimal aerodynamic drag.

ANGLE OF ATTACK

Not all passes gracefully turn over in this way, though. The passes that don't do so tend to be launched at high-trajectory angles and with overly positive angles of attack. The gyroscopic effect keeps the spin axis in a constant angle of inclination, and on descent the ball will assume an even greater angle of attack. With a far greater lift and torque than in an ideal orientation, the result is precession, or a wobbling, of the football's spin axis.

A great quarterback might very well instinctively also use factors such as angle of attack to control the ball's flight.

"These are things we might measure after a quarterback has developed his particular technique through trial and error," says Sforza. "For a great quarterback, minor adjustments in headwinds or tailwinds or crosswinds, or getting a little extra hang time by using a slightly greater positive angle of attack, are second nature, a subconscious talent."

CONTROLLING THE THROW

Considering the precision that a good pass requires, the football seems almost designed to resist throwing. To control spin and orientation, the hand needs to be close to the center of gravity, that is, near the ball's middle. However, to generate sufficient velocity, the hand's force needs to come from behind, in other words, as far back as possible.

The resulting grip represents a compromise. A quarterback will hold the ball as far back as he can while still far enough forward to maintain control.

Throwing a football well requires the player to make a cumbersome object behave in a variety of ways. Beyond finding the right balance of direction and velocity, the quarterback must control spin and orientation. It's little wonder the experts rate the bomb high on a list of quarterback duties.

"The bomb is one of the most delicate passes a quarterback has to throw," said the late Sid Gillman, a coaching veteran of 27 collegiate and 25 professional seasons. "You've got to throw it not just with distance but also trajectory. It's got to be laid up there and timed perfectly."

Gillman worked for five NFL teams and was head coach of the San Diego Chargers for twelve years. Many consider him the pioneer of the passing game in the NFL, which inducted him into the Pro Football Hall of Fame in 1983.

"What you're doing, if you have a productive deep passing game, is stretching the field," said Gillman, who saw the long ball as both tactical and psychological weapon. "And I mean a productive game. Defenders start to worry about getting beat deep."

Both Gillman and Shula are careful to distinguish between the true bomb and plays that rely on a little bit of luck. For instance, the long, desperate play known as the "Hail Mary" can be mistaken for a bomb because it goes so far, but as a pass it is basically a heave.

"The bomb is tougher to complete, but the rewards are greater," says Shula. "A quick in or a quick out is easier to execute, but it gains under 10 yards. You can use it to keep your drive going. You hit the bombs and it's 50 or 60 yards and a touchdown." His former quarterback agrees.

"I think a quarterback gets a feeling of excitement when the long bomb is completed," says Marino.

The beauty of football is its coordinated action, and the long pass is an impressive expression of just that—two players, widely separated, connecting their efforts with the high flight of a pass rising from the finesse to drop . . . just like a bomb.

KICKING A FIELD GOAL

by MATT BAHR

This article was published in POPULAR MECHANICS in 1992.

ONE OF THE
GREAT PARADOXES
OF FOOTBALL IS
THAT THE PLAYER
WHO SPENDS THE
LEAST AMOUNT OF
TIME ON THE FIELD
IS THE PLAYER WHO
OFTEN DETERMINES
WHETHER HIS
TEAM GOES HOME A
WINNER OR A LOSER
AFTER THE GAME.

Kickers, it can be argued, may have become unintentionally prominent on the field, and perhaps some of the original spirit of the game has been lost due to the impact kickers can have on the outcome of a contest. As the game stands now, though, there will be many instances during the course of the season when all eyes will be focused on the kicker.

THE CENTER AND THE HOLDER

Yet a kicker is only one cog in a well-oiled machine that performs its job in 1.2 seconds. The other key elements in the equation are the center's snap, the hold, and the protection. Without these, there's no kick.

Centers are offensive linemen who can pass the ball like an upside-down quarterback and then be immediately blasted by a defender. For a field goal, the center snaps the ball backward seven to eight yards, depending upon the kicker's preference and how quickly he can elevate the ball. As the ball reaches the holder it should be still on the rise. The snap has to have pace, but it can't be hiked so hard that the holder has to fight to hold it. Most

◄ Matt Bahr of the New York Giants kicks a field goal during Super Bowl XXV against the Buffalo Bills at Tampa Stadium in Tampa, Florida, in 1991. The Giants won the game, 20–19.

▶ Hungarian-born Pete Gogolak is credited with popularizing soccer-style kicking. Gogolak (Buffalo, 1964–65; New York Giants, 1966–74) led the American Football League in field goals in 1965, scoring 115 points.

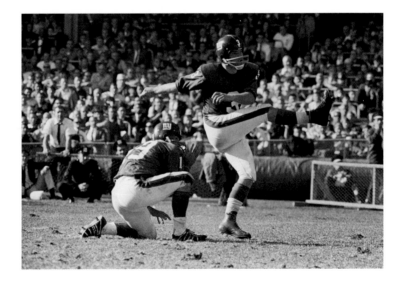

NFL centers are able to snap the ball so that the laces are facing forward when it reaches the holder.

The holder, meanwhile, wants to meet the ball and bring it down with him. The best position in which to catch the ball is with the back knee up and the front knee down. In this position, the holder can move to the ball if the snap is off without getting out of position. The back knee acts as a backstop and also as a guide for positioning the ball. Holding the ball with the left hand (for a right-footed kicker) allows the holder to spin the ball laces forward if necessary with his right hand. The laces of the ball should always face forward—laces facing toward either side will make the ball curve in that direction. This also gives the kicker a good view of the ball. Quarterbacks tend to be the best holders because they handle the ball the most and have an even temperament. A calm holder keeps the kicker calm.

KICK STYLES

All NFL kickers use a soccer-style approach, meaning they come at the ball from a 45-degree angle. Soccer-style kickers dominate the league because they are more accurate than straight-on kickers. The accuracy comes from getting more of the foot's surface area on the ball. A soccer-style kicker hits the ball with a larger rectangular area of the foot, as opposed to a single point. Your foot also doesn't have to be angled as severely to hit the ball correctly.

One great exception, of course, is Tom Dempsey, formerly of the New Orleans Saints and holder of the record for the longest field goal at 63 yards. While Dempsey kicked straight-on, his club

Tom Dempsey of the New Orleans Saints walloped the ball for a record 63-yard field goal on November 8, 1970, against the Detroit Lions.

foot was like a war mallet, affording him plenty of surface contact with the ball (see photograph on previous page). Note: Jason Elam of the Denver Broncos, a soccer-style kicker, tied Dempsey's record in 1998 as have Sebastian Janikowski of the Oakland Raiders (2011) and David Akers of the San Francisco 49ers (2012). Today, the only straight-on kickers in the NFL are emergency backup kickers who normally play other positions.

THE PLAY

Remember, the holder positions the ball seven yards behind the line of scrimmage, eight yards if the kicker drives the ball. The kicker assumes, however, that the offensive line will be pushed back two yards. This means the ball must rise ten feet—the height of a lineman with his arms extended upward—within five yards, or fifteen feet. Placing the ball farther back allows the world-class sprinter at the end of the defensive line to run in a straight line to block the kick. Forcing the defensive cornerman to run at the ball in a bow pattern slows him down. The idea is to get as far away from the line of scrimmage as possible without giving the defensive corner a line to run on. A fast defensive cornerman can run to the block point in 1.4 seconds. That's why you practice kicking in 1.2 seconds. At 1.3 seconds, a kicker is pushing the ragged edge. At 1.4 seconds, you eat the ball.

I start my move to the ball as soon as it hits the holder's hands. For me, it's two steps and a little hop to get the motion going. As I approach the ball, my supporting leg is planted a foot's length away from the ball. You should be able to draw a straight line from the ball to a point between the arch and the heel of the planted foot. The toes of the planted foot are pointed at the target, the target being some point through and beyond the goalposts. Your body weight is over the ball, and this puts you in position to maximize your follow-through.

▲ Soccer-style kickers approach the ball from a 45-degree angle. The planted foot, which points toward the target, is a foot-length away from the ball as the kicking foot makes contact. The ball is kicked toe-down on the upper part of the shoelaces. A quick skip keeps the hips from turning. Forward momentum, therefore, stays directed at the target. Hips and shoulders are aligned toward the target during the follow-through.

▲ The contact point is the football's sweet spot one inch below the center of the axis of the ball.

MECHANICS OF THE KICK

The best place to hit the ball is in the sweet spot just below the center of the ball. When I make contact, I'm hitting the sweet spot with the top part of my foot—on the shoelaces—with my toe pointing downward. The ball goes up, not because you're lifting it, but because you're hitting it just below the center axis.

For me to hit the sweet spot effectively, the holder should position the ball at about a 5-degree angle toward his body rather than straight up and down. Because of the angle at which your foot is hitting the ball, this slight tilt actually creates a more perpendicular alignment between the foot and the ball. This positioning reduces the tendency of the ball to hook off-target while it's in the air. Footballs hook when your hips and shoulders open up too much and your kicking foot comes across the ball.

Hitting the ball with the laces forward is ideal. Hitting the ball with the laces facing back is almost as good. Of course, with the laces back, you don't get the desired compression of the ball, because the laces are in the way. Laces facing to either side screw up the ball's rotation. With the laces to the side, the mass of the ball shifts, as does the position of the sweet spot.

Older balls are better to kick than new balls. With wear and tear, the ball becomes a balloon. It becomes easier to kick because there's more compression and it goes farther. In a game, every ball is new, but the home-team ball boys will give an official a ball that is a little less new than the others. The difference between kicking a new ball and an older ball may mean as much as an extra ten yards in distance. Every little bit helps.

As I'm planting my left foot, my kicking leg is already cocked—so much so that it looks as if I'm kicking myself in the back. The knee is bent at a 45-degree angle, and the lower portion of the leg is virtually parallel to the ground. By bending the knee and whipping your leg toward the ball, you get the foot speed necessary to kick the ball for distance. For a split second, neither of my feet is on the ground. My kicking leg has to be cocked before the other leg is planted because there is no time to do it any other way.

As I'm planting my foot, the holder is putting down the ball. During the kick, the lower back and the stomach muscles are moving toward the ball even before my foot is.

I'm more of a mechanical kicker than a natural kicker. This means I try to do the same thing every time whether it's a 45-yard field goal or an extra point. There are no chip shots.

The difference between a natural kicker and a mechanical

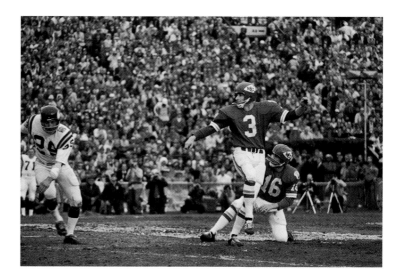

Kansas City kicker Jan Stenerud and quarterback Len Dawson watch as Stenerud's 48-yard field goal passes through the uprights during the first quarter of Super Bowl IV at Tulane Stadium in New Orleans, Louisiana, on January 11, 1970. The 48-yard kick was a Super Bowl record.

kicker is most evident during the follow-through. A natural kicker will add a little distance by turning his hips away from the target after contact. I work on taking my hips all the way through the kick. However, I stop my hips from turning and instead direct my momentum toward the target. At this point, I'm skipping through the ball and my left ankle looks as if it will break if I come down on it. The hop prevents me from spinning and keeps me aligned toward the target. This way, if I mis-hit the ball, the momentum of the follow-through still gives me a chance to make the field goal. By contrast, when a natural kicker mis-hits the ball, you'll see an audacious hook or a lot of rotation because he's under the ball or because it slid off his foot.

As a kicker, you want the ball to have a slow rotation. You can tell from the rotation where the ball was kicked. Hit the sweet spot and you'll see a slow end-over-end rotation. If the ball spins like a top, then the kicker has hit way under the sweet spot.

A KICKER'S ENEMIES

At one time, kickers had to worry about things like leapers—defensive players who took a running start from behind the line of scrimmage and then jumped into the air. Offensive linemen bet on whether they could make leapers do a 360-degree or 540-degree spin in the air. To prevent injuries, the defense is no longer allowed to jump from behind the line of scrimmage.

Today, a kicker's biggest adversary is the weather. Cold weather can cut your range by five to ten yards because you don't get as much compression of the ball as you kick. Wet weather forces you to shorten your stride to avoid slipping. The biggest problem, though, is the wind.

The wind can kill your kick, but you never want to choose a target that would take the ball on a natural trajectory outside the goalposts. The wind can die just as quickly as it starts up.

A wind coming straight at the kicker will kill the ball distance-wise, but it doesn't push the ball to either side. A wind coming from the left doesn't cause many problems because you're kicking through a cross section.

However, a wind coming diagonally from the right is murder because if you have any hook on the ball, the wind will exaggerate it—pushing the ball too far to the left. If you hit into the wind you won't get any hook, but you'll miss to the right. Under the circumstances, making an accurate kick is very difficult.

The wind does help if you have it at your back. You'll get about three-quarters of the range that you lose with the wind in your face.

Let's say I can normally make a 50-yard field goal. If a strong wind is in my face, it will reduce my range to about 40 yards. With the wind at my back, my range will increase about 7.5 yards, so there's a chance I will make a 57-yarder.

Adversity is part of the game, so it can't be offered as an excuse for a missed field goal. Kickers are always about three misses away from retirement. The key to longevity is to kick the ball in a natural and comfortable way with as much leg speed and accuracy as you can muster.

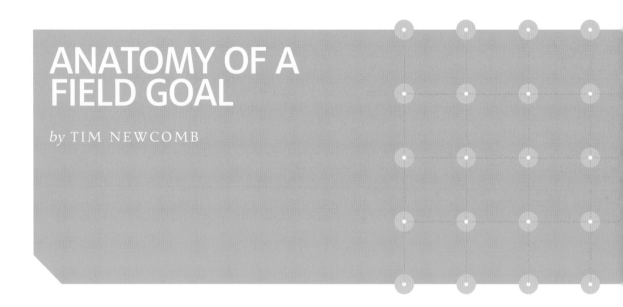

ANATOMY OF A FIELD GOAL

by TIM NEWCOMB

1. THE HOLD

Everyone knows the laces should point away from the kicker's foot, but pros like Henery demand that the ball be standing straight up too. Tilting it lowers the center of mass, making it tougher to strike the sweet spot, says biomechanics professor Jeff Hawks, who studied Henery's technique with colleague Chase Pfeifer at the University of Nebraska, Lincoln.

2. THE PLANT

During his approach, Henery places his left foot, heel first, next to the ball—barely 10 inches from the nose. By positioning himself this close and pointing his planted big toe directly at the goalpost, the kicker opens his hips and draws power from the core muscles in his torso and legs.

3. THE ARM

The 177-pound pro extends his left arm at a 90-degree angle, keeping his body in balance as his chest and hips face the target. While leg speed is crucial for distance, posture and balance dictate accuracy, says Sacramento State professor of kinesiology David Mandeville.

4. THE KICK

Any misplaced movement reduces velocity and energy. Henery strikes the sweet spot with the top of his foot ("right where you

tie your shoes," he says) and powers straight on through it. When he makes contact with the ball, his foot is traveling 53 to 60 mph. By accelerating through the ball, he squeezes every bit of power from his upright kicking motion. The sweeping follow-through lets his foot reach peak speed in the 0.03 seconds after contact.

THE FLIGHT OF THE BALL

As a sophomore at the University of Nebraska, Henery once kicked a 57-yard field goal. He made it look easy—and that's the whole point. When kickers break form, they get into trouble. With a perfect strike and no wasted energy, Henery can launch the ball at a velocity of 53 mph and 1400 rpm. The faster the rotation, the less drag the ball will encounter. If he tried to put more leg into the kick, odds are good he'd send the ball off on the wrong trajectory. According to Rodney Imamura, who researched kicks alongside David Mandeville and Michael Nave at Sacramento State, field goal attempts generally soar at an angle between 27 and 42 degrees. Henery's kicks are more precise, leaving his foot in the safe range between 31 and 41 degrees.

JUST ONE KICK IS ALL IT TOOK

by PETER BRANCAZIO

Since a football is not perfectly round, the aerodynamic forces influencing its flight depend significantly on the alignment of the football's axis with respect to its path toward the target.

For a field-goal kicker, getting the football to spiral nose first is impossible. The best alternative is to make it spin end-over-end around a side-to-side axis. While the aerodynamic drag is greater than it would be for a spiral, the ball will at least have a gyroscopic action, giving its spin axis a constant direction in space. On an ideal end-over-end kick, the spin axis of the ball should be horizontal and parallel to the yard lines as the ball travels toward the goalpost. If there's no wind, the ball will not drift or curve sideways.

To achieve maximum distance, a field-goal kicker should launch the kick at about a 45-degree angle. To prevent the kick from being blocked, the ball should be at least ten feet above the ground two yards before the original line of scrimmage. This is ensured if the kick is launched at an angle of 35 degrees or more. Finally, the ball must be hit with enough force to clear the crossbar, ten feet above the ground. This means the actual landing point of the trajectory must be at least three or four yards past the goalpost.

Professional field-goal kickers are frequently called upon to perform this difficult task under exceptional pressure in the closing seconds of the game with a win—or even the championship—on the line.

One of the classic examples is Matt Bahr's 42-yard field goal that sent the New York Giants to Super Bowl XXV in 1991. Bahr's kick was straight and true, with a perfect end-over-end rotation, and with three seconds on the clock, the Giants defeated the San Francisco 49ers for the NFC Championship.

A close examination of the videotape showed that Bahr's kick cleared the crossbar by a considerable margin, landing about twelve yards behind the goalposts. Thus, the overall distance was about 54 yards. The hang time was 3.6 seconds. A computer simulation, taking the effects of air resistance into account, indicates the kick was probably launched with an initial speed of about 65 mph, at an angle close to 45 degrees.

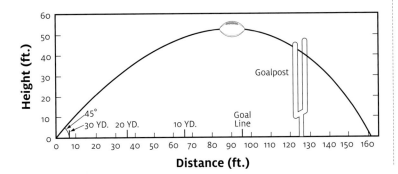

144

BATTLE HELMETS

by ANDREW GAFFNEY

WHEN YOU STRAP ON A FOOTBALL HELMET, PART OF YOU FEELS AS IF YOU'RE GOING TO WAR, LIKE SOME MEDIEVAL KNIGHT OF OLD ABOUT TO WAGE HAND-TO-HAND COMBAT. THE REALITY IS THAT FOOTBALL IS JUST A GAME, BUT ONE THAT COMES WITH THE RISK OF PHYSICAL INJURY. THAT'S WHY THE PLAYERS WEAR HELMETS.

It's no secret that quarterbacks Troy Aikman of the Dallas Cowboys and Steve Young of the San Francisco 49ers retired because of repeated head injuries. Their departure focused more attention on helmets and the need to further protect players against debilitating and life-threatening concussions.

In 2002, Riddell developed a new Revolution helmet designed to reduce the incidence of concussion. Schutt Sports Group, the other major helmet manufacturer, followed suit with an improved helmet of its own called DNA. A three-year, Riddell-financed study of high-school players by the University of Pittsburgh Medical Center found that the annual rate of concussion was 5.3 percent for players wearing the Revolution helmet and 7.6 percent for players wearing standard helmets.

While no helmet can prevent a concussion, these helmets offer a protection level that is unprecedented. It's been only 70 years since helmets were made mandatory in the NFL and in colleges. In fact, former President Gerald Ford was one of those players who braved the game without a helmet, in the early 1930s, as a center for the Michigan Wolverines. And while that opened the door for a lot of one-liners about the need for helmets, that little tidbit does illustrate how far head protection has come in the interim.

HELMET HISTORY

Although helmets did not become standard gear until after World War II, some pioneering players wore primitive head covering as far back as the early 1900s. The earliest versions, called "head harnesses," were made of soft leather and were predominantly designed to cover the ears. Because the flaps on the original head harnesses covered the ear completely, however, they were criticized for hindering communication on the playing field.

The first helmets offering full protection of the skull and featuring holes in the earflaps were introduced between 1915 and 1917. Although the flat-top caps were still made of soft leather, they offered some suspension, rather than resting directly on the skull.

During the 1920s and 1930s, makers began to utilize harder leathers and some fabric cushioning for greater protection.

◀ Cincinnati Bengals and Indianapolis Colts players at the line of scrimmage prior to the snap during the game at the RCA Dome in Indianapolis, Indiana, in December 2006. The Colts defeated the Bengals 34–16.

Helmets also began evolving from the flat-top shape, adopting more of the teardrop shape of the skull and allowing the impact of a blow to slide to one side rather than being absorbed head-on.

The granddaddy of helmet innovation, however, came in 1939, when the John T. Riddell Company of Chicago introduced the first plastic football helmet. In addition to being stronger than leather models, the plastic helmet proved to be more durable. Riddell is credited with adding the first face mask, also plastic, in 1940 and moving the helmet strap from the Adam's apple to the chin.

Despite its performance improvements, the plastic helmet did have to overcome some hurdles before it would drastically change the game. Because plastics and other materials were scarce during World War II, some of Riddell's early models were not particularly well made. In fact, after Fred Naumetz of the Los Angeles Rams split nine in one season, plastic helmets were banned from the NFL. (Meanwhile, that same year, Fred Gehrke, another Rams player, and a former art student, became the first to paint a team logo on his helmet.)

Riddell quickly made some refinements in the types of synthetics used for construction, and with some lobbying from coach George Halas of the Chicago Bears, plastic helmets were reinstated in 1949 and soon after became the official helmets of the NFL. Riddell's earliest molded shells still serve as models for modern energy-absorbing helmets, which feature specially molded polycarbon plastic construction and high-tech cushioning systems.

Face masks evolved along the same lines—with early versions often shattering—until the development of the tubular bar in 1955. Popularized by legendary Cleveland Browns quarterback Otto Graham, the single bar soon blossomed into the vertical birdcage worn by today's players. Dark visors were added in the mid-1980s for use by players with eye injuries.

OTHER INNOVATIONS

While a number of innovations—including a one-piece system designed to replace the conventional helmet, shoulder pads, and rib guard—were proposed, one that stuck is the ProCap from Protective Sports Equipment, in Erie, Pennsylvania. The ProCap is basically a polyurethane semi-hard pad that attaches to the outside of a standard football helmet. Buffalo Bills trainer Ed Abramowski first recommended the pad to safety Mark Kelso in 1990 after he had suffered a string of concussions. Kelso went

Early 1900s
Soft leather harness style. YMCA team from Latrobe, Pennsylvania.

1915
Soft leather flat-top style. Typical of early pro team Canton Bulldogs.

1920s
Soft leather helmet. Typical of the NFL's Duluth Eskimos.

1930s, early 1940s
Hard leather style. Typical of the NFL's Chicago Bears.

1940s
Hard leather, first graphics. Los Angeles Rams.

1950s, 1960s
Plastic helmet. Detroit Lions.

1970s, early 1980s
Plastic helmet. St. Louis Cardinals.

1980s to present
Plastic helmet. Minnesota Vikings.

Riddell Revolution helmet.

ProCap, a polyurethane pad that attaches to the outside of the helmet, is an added safeguard against concussions.

🔺 The Evolution of the Helmet

on to play five more seasons with the ProCap and became such a supporter of the product that he predicted it will "one day be the standard in the helmet industry." In addition to Kelso, Steve Wallace, an offensive tackle with the San Francisco 49ers, was an early adopter, wearing it in the 1995 Super Bowl. The product became widely used in youth, high school, and college programs.

ProCap was designed by Bert Strauss, a former industrial-design consultant, who saw the need for more protection from concussions and other head injuries. Strauss claimed that the ProCap absorbed 30 percent more energy than whatever helmet it sits on, reducing the impact and trauma to the head. Strauss compared ProCap to softer car bumpers.

Riddell and Schutt Sports Group still dominate the football helmet trade. Riddell's new Revolution helmet is the biggest structural change in helmet design in a generation. After research showed that 70 percent of concussions were the result of side impact, Riddell extended the helmet shell to cover the jaw area. The company also included an inflatable padding system for a more custom fit and used computer software to design the helmet around the head's center of gravity. The distance between the helmet shell and the interior pads was increased and the face guard was isolated to reduce jarring to the shell from face guard collisions. Fullback James Hodgins of the St. Louis Rams became the first player to wear a Revolution helmet, in Super Bowl XXXVI. Schutt responded with a new DNA helmet that uses a shock-absorbing plastic material called Skydex, the same material used to protect the heads of Army paratroopers and Navy SEALs.

The future may lie in radio telemetry. Numerous college teams are experimenting with Riddell's Head Impact Telemetry (HIT) System, which alerts sideline coaches when a preset impact threshold has been reached for an individual player. Six small sensors, similar to those that trigger airbags in cars, are inserted in the player's helmet. Impact data is transmitted wirelessly to a computer on the sideline.

Thankfully, there is no going back to the day when Ivy Leaguers grew their hair long to protect themselves from head injuries. Smart technology wins out over toughness, even on the gridiron.

HEAD GAMES: HOW HELMET TECH WORKS IN 7 DIFFERENT SPORTS

by JOE P. HASLER

A brain may be a terrible thing to waste, but that hasn't stopped legions of athletes from stepping onto the football field to bang heads in pursuit of gridiron glory. Football players are notoriously stubborn when it comes to protecting (or not protecting) their noggins. Even the invention of the football helmet, credited by some to Navy midshipman Joseph Reeves, came as an act of defiance to medical warnings. Before the Army-Navy game in 1893, a Navy doctor told Reeves, who would go on to become the "Father of Carrier Aviation," that one more blow to the head might result in death or insanity. Rather than miss a date with his rival servicemen, Reeves enlisted the help of a cobbler to fashion a rudimentary helmet made of leather straps. Navy won the game 6–4, and Reeves survived his playing career.

More recently, doctors have backed up their cautionary words with studies establishing a strong link between repeated concussions and cognitive impairment. And late last month the National Football League—after a lengthy review of how its teams handle head injuries—enacted an immediate policy change regarding concussions. The new rules prohibit players who experience concussion-like symptoms (memory loss, dizziness) from returning to the game. Previously, only players knocked unconscious were banned from resuming play. With all the attention athletic head injuries are attracting, PM decided to survey the myriad playing fields to find out what's considered state-of-the-art when it comes to skull safety.

FOOTBALL
When Riddell unveiled its Revolution model in 2002, it was the first major advance in football headgear technology in a quarter-century, and the first helmet designed specifically to reduce concussions. The major innovation of the Revolution is its exterior shell, dubbed the Tru-Curve. This new shell provides increased coverage on the side of the head, along the jaw line. Riddell claims players who wear the Revolution are 30 percent less susceptible to concussions.

Yet even with its innovations, the Revolution sticks to the standard football-helmet format of a polycarbonate shell with internal foam padding that Riddell first introduced 70 years ago. The truly revolutionary football helmet might be the Xenith X1, conceived by former Harvard quarterback Vin Ferrara, which ditches the foam padding. Instead, the X1 relies on an internal system called the Shock Bonnet. The flexible bonnet conforms to the wearer's head and is separated from the external plastic shell by a set of 18 hollow thermoplastic shock absorbers. On impact these puck-shaped devices compress to absorb the energy of the hit. Theoretically, this reduces the jarring of the head inside the helmet, thus reducing the likelihood of brain injuries.

SKIING & SNOWBOARDING
The jury remains out on helmet's effectiveness in preventing serious brain injuries on the slopes. According to the National

Ski Areas Association (NSAA), during the 2008–09 ski season, nearly half of all skiers and in the United States wore helmets, an increase of almost 25 percent from 2002–03. Yet even as helmet use increased, the number of skiing-related deaths has remained steady. Dave Byrd, the NSAA's director of education and risk, told the Santa Fe New Mexican that for skiers traveling at speeds in excess of 14 mph, which most do, a helmet is unlikely to make much difference.

The efficacy debate notwithstanding, ski and snowboard helmet-tech development has marched on, and those who do opt for headgear have a plethora of lightweight and streamlined models from which to choose. State-of-the-art consumer models from manufacturers such as Giro and Uvex are made from polycarbonate shells molded with shock-absorbing polystyrene foam. This "in-mold" construction eliminates the need for glued-in padding. Helmet makers have also created models that integrate not only goggles, but also personal audio systems with tiny speakers built into earpieces.

But that only pertains to recreational skiers.

Professionals seem damned if they do, damned if they don't. The International Ski Federation mandates that all competitors wear helmets that conform to rigorous standards, but traveling at speeds sometimes exceeding 75 mph on rock-hard, icy courses, downhill ski racers are particularly prone to horrific head injuries, even with helmets. Wearing a helmet, for example, didn't prevent Swiss downhiller Daniel Albrecht from ending up in a three-week coma last January after he crashed while racing in Austria.

BASEBALL

A traditional batting helmet, comprising a hard ABS plastic shell encasing soft foam padding, is engineered to withstand baseball

impacts at speeds of up to 70 mph. Considering the average Major League fastball zips in at closer to 90 mph, one might expect professional baseball players to readily accept Rawlings' S100, the first batting helmet designed to protect against high-speed pitches to the head. That wasn't the case, though.

The S100, which has an interior made of multiple layers of expanded polypropylene instead of soft foam, was first introduced toward the end of the 2009 season. Most of the players who tested it—including the Mets star David Wright, who did so after being struck in the head by a pitch—complained that the new model was too bulky, and an uncomfortable

distraction when batting and running the bases. Wright abandoned the S100 for his old helmet after just two games.

Rawlings then developed the S100 Pro Comp model. The new streamlined helmet, made with carbon fiber instead of plastic, is both smaller and nearly five ounces lighter than the 2009 model. Beginning in 2013, all major leaguers were required to wear the new helmet. The only exceptions are players (generally switch-hitters) who wear helmets with earflaps on both sides. About 200 players had already switched to the new helmet during the 2012 season.

CYCLING

The basic composition of standard-issue bicycle helmets hasn't changed much in the last quarter-century, though the same can't be said of style and design. In the mid-1970s, Bell unveiled the Biker, which featured an interior lining made of crushable expanded polystyrene (EPS) encased in a hard Lexan plastic shell. To this day, the majority of bike helmets—including those worn on most race days of the Tour de France, since the UCI (cycling's governing body) mandated helmet use in 2005—are made from EPS, though Lexan has been replaced by thinner and lighter polycarbonate shells.

High-end helmets like the $230 Giro Ionos, which boasts a whooping 21 air vents (and is worn by Lance Armstrong), are made using the so-called in-mold production method. This means the EPS is basically cooked into its polycarbonate shell during production, which allows for a lighter product. The major drawback of EPS helmets is that they can only sustain one impact. After that, the foam lining is crushed, and the helmet is useless.

ICE HOCKEY

Considering the various factors that make up the game of hockey—a frozen playing surface, a hard rubber puck traveling at high speeds, sharp skate blades, body checks and stick-wielding competitors—helmet use seems like it should be a given. Yet it wasn't until 1979 that the National Hockey League made protective headgear compulsory. Goaltenders on the professional level didn't begin regularly wearing face masks until 1960, when Montreal Canadiens' goalie Jacques Plante started the trend. After having his face ripped open during a 1959 game against New York, Plante—who had previously fractured his jaw, nose and skull—was able to convince his coach to allow him onto the ice wearing a custom-made fiberglass mask (à la Friday the 13th's Jason).

Goalie tech has come a long way since Plante's rudimentary, yet revolutionary, safety measure. These days the mode in masks is the so-called hybrid mask, also known as the mage-style (mask + cage). Top-shelf masks from makers like Warwick and Sportmask combine resilient shells made of high-grade fiberglass and resin with a steel face-guarding cage and interior foam padding that absorbs impact.

EQUESTRIAN

It's a long fall from the top of a horse to the ground below. Add in the element of a leaping steed, and the seemingly genteel sport of the equestrian begins to seem almost extreme. When one thinks of equestrian headgear, though, it's usually the velveteen-covered foxhunt-style cap that comes to mind. For all its classy styling, the thin, plastic-shell "hard hat" was practically useless as a safety precaution.

In the early 1990s, riding-headgear makers took a cue from bike helmets and for the first time employed shock-absorbing foam linings. These bulky originals were slow to catch on with competitive riders and the public. It wasn't until manufacturers such as San Diego–based Troxel, starting slimming down their products to resemble the old-style hats that protective headgear became de rigueur. Today, riding helmets consist of impact-negating foam paired with external shells made from hard plastics, carbon fiber, or more traditional materials like velvet or suede.

AUTORACING

In the 1980s, Bill Hubbard, a biomechanical engineering professor at Michigan State, set about designing a device that would protect automotive racers from the dreaded basal skull fracture. This potentially fatal injury occurs when the head is rattled so violently that the skull literally snaps off the spine, and it is unfortunately common among race-car drivers. During an 18-month period in 2000 and 2001, four Nascar drivers, including the legendary Dale Earnhardt, died from the injury.

Tragic as it was, Earnhardt's death represented a crucial moment for racing safety, as it prompted much soul searching in the sport and led to widespread adoption of Hubbard's creation, the Head and Neck Support (HANS) device. Like a pair of football shoulder pads, the device slips around the driver's neck (imagine a tall collar made of Kevlar and carbon fiber), then attaches to the driver's helmet, so that the head and body move as one in a crash. In 2001, after Earnhardt's crash, Nascar mandated that all racers use head and neck restraints, and since then the series has experienced zero fatalities according to the *Miami Herald*.

ANATOMY OF
A HIT

by MATT HIGGINS

IT HAPPENS ABOUT 100 TIMES A GAME IN THE NATIONAL FOOTBALL LEAGUE: A BONE-JARRING TACKLE THAT SLAMS A PLAYER TO THE TURF. INCOMPLETIONS AND FUMBLES AREN'T THE ONLY CONSEQUENCES OF SUCH TACKLES— MORE THAN 100 CONCUSSIONS ARE RECORDED EACH SEASON IN THE NFL.

Given the size and speed of today's athletes, it's surprising that more gridiron warriors aren't carried off the field on their shields. For that, they can thank high-tech gear that protects them from the physics at play in the sport's fearsome collisions.

HALF A TON OF HURT

At 5-foot-11 and 199 pounds, the Marcus Trufant, now with the Jacksonville Jaguars is an average-size NFL defensive back (DB). Those stats don't stand out in a league where more than 500 players weighed 300-plus pounds at the 2006 training camps. But a DB's mass combined with his speed—on average, 4.56 seconds for the 40-yard dash—can produce up to 1,600 pounds of tackling force, according to Timothy Gay, a physics professor at the University of Nebraska and author of *The Physics of Football*.

A tackle with more than half a ton of force sounds like a crippling blow. But, according to John Melvin, an injury biomechanics researcher for General Motors and NASCAR, the body can handle twice that amount—as long as the impact is well distributed. That job usually is handled by the player's equipment, which spreads out the incoming energy, lessening its severity.

BODY ARMOR

Shoulder-pad plastic hasn't changed much in 30 years, but it is now molded into designs with more right angles to deflect impacts. Players also rely on the helmet's solid shell and face mask to redistribute the energy of a collision.

During a tackle, foam padding beneath the plastic components of equipment compresses, absorbing energy and reducing the speed of impact. (The slower a hit, the less force it generates.) Visco elastic foam, which was invented by NASA to protect astronauts from g-forces during liftoff, retains its shape better than conventional foam, rebounding rapidly after hits.

According to a Virginia Tech study, a tackle like Trufant's in the photo at left probably caused Philadelphia Eagles receiver Greg Lewis's head to accelerate in his helmet at 30 to 60 g's. VT researchers gather data with the Head Impact Telemetry System, which employs sensors and wireless transmitters in helmets. "We

◀ Seattle Seahawks defensive back Marcus Trufant (23) drilled Philadelphia Eagles receiver Greg Lewis (83) with such force that Lewis couldn't hang on to the ball. Seattle won the December 5, 2005, game at Philadelphia 42–0 in the most lopsided shutout ever broadcast on *Monday Night Football*.

see 100-g impacts all the time," says Stefan Duma, director of the university's Center for Injury Biomechanics, "and several over 150 g's."

While Trufant and Lewis, who retired in 2010, generally enjoyed healthy careers, they (and other players) face the same nemesis: the dreaded knee injury. The knee's anterior cruciate ligament can withstand nearly 500 pounds of pressure, but it tears far more easily from side hits and evasive maneuvers. According to the *Pittsburgh Tribune-Review*, more than 1,200 knee injuries were reported by the league between 2000 and 2003, accounting for one out of every six injuries—by far the highest percentage in the NFL.

HITTING THE DECK

Researchers rate a field's shock absorbency with a metric called G-Max. To measure it, an object that approximates a human head and neck (about twenty square inches and twenty pounds) is dropped from a height of two feet. A low G-Max means the field absorbs more energy than the player. Trufant and Lewis landed on grass in Philly's new stadium, which has a cushy G-Max of just over 60. Synthetic surfaces have G-Max ratings of up to 120. The hardest turf: frozen grass.

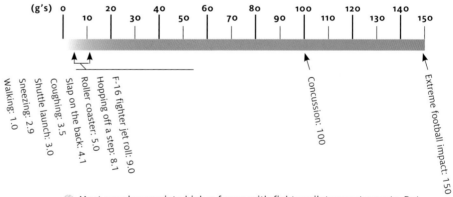

Most people associate high g-forces with fighter pilots or astronauts. But common earthbound events can also boost g's. Few things can match the g-load of a wicked football hit.

Golf

THE SEARCH FOR THE PERFECT GOLF SWING

by TY WENGER

IS THERE A SECRET TO ACHIEVING THE PERFECT SWING? KNOWING THE PHYSICS—AND EMPLOYING THE PROPER FUNDAMENTALS—CAN HELP UNCOVER IT.

Jack Nicklaus utilized an upright, over-the-top power fade. Arnold Palmer employed an animalistic, knee-buckling, inside-out slash. Lee Trevino aimed far to the left and sliced the ball around the course. The great Byron Nelson squatted forward like a tourist performing a hula dance.

Butch Harmon, the man who helped construct the swing that Tiger Woods used to dominate professional golf at the turn of the century, preaches the benefits of an upright "two-plane" approach. Hank Haney, the man who helped ruin and then re-build the swing that Tiger used to dominate professional golf until he was replaced by Sean Foley, evangelizes on behalf of a flat "one-plane" method. Foley teaches a "stack and hit" swing technique.

Mike Austin, the legendary kinesiology expert credited with striking the longest drive in PGA Tour history—515 yards, *at the age of 64*—claimed that his "secret" was a forward press of the wrists, coupled with a forceful lateral shift of the hips and the casting of the club. Instructor John Novosel claims that a tempo of three beats (in the backswing) to one beat (in the downswing) is "golf's last secret," a panacea for all that ails any swing. Ben Hogan claimed to have discovered a mysterious, mythical "secret" to his swing—which, being Hogan, he never fully revealed.

Each of these men is right.

And every one of them is wrong.

Because there is, in truth, no such thing as the perfect golf swing.

Indeed, part of the reason that Hogan never fully revealed his secret (other than the fact that he was a vicious competitor who would have sooner eaten his golf tees than hand his competitors the benefit of his knowledge) was that he believed his secret (essentially, a pronation of his wrists at the top of his backswing that eliminated, for him, the dreaded pull-hook) was all but useless to anyone else. All golf swings are necessary extensions of the body employing them. And as with snowflakes and spiderwebs, no two bodies—hence no two swings—are ever exactly alike. The real secret, Hogan often said, could be found in the dirt. You've got to dig it out yourself.

At its simplest, the ultimate goal of the golf swing is merely this: deliver the club to the ball, at a high rate of speed, with the

◄ The "Great White Shark," Greg Norman, finished first on the PGA tour twenty times before retiring in 2005.

Whether it's the inside-out slash used by Arnold Palmer (left) or the over-the-top power swing favored by Jack Nicklaus (right), great players tend to develop their own signature swing. Here, Palmer is playing at The Masters in 1965 at the Augusta National Golf Club in Augusta, Georgia; Nicklaus is shown playing in 1981.

clubface square to the target and moving, at impact, on a path directly through the ball. The point is that—to a certain degree—everything that happens prior to impact and directly after impact is, in a way, irrelevant. In truth, a golfer can swing the club from his knees (actually a useful training drill), or with a running approach (like, say, Happy Gilmore), or by eliminating the backswing altogether (as Johnny Miller experimented with back in the 1970s), so long as he can consistently and repeatedly throw the center of that clubface through the ball.

Then again, knowing the physics of the swing—and employing the proper fundamentals—makes the job all the easier. Perhaps you remember from tenth-grade physics that kinetic energy = $\frac{1}{2}$ mass X velocity^2. From the standpoint of pure physics, how much energy the club has when it collides with the ball therefore depends on only two things: the mass of the club and, far more importantly, its speed in a particular direction, or velocity. The goal of the golf swing, then, is to retain the potential energy of your club until it's converted into kinetic energy at the moment of contact with the ball. Your swing is a machine. It can be either a highly efficient one (see: Tiger Woods) or a highly inefficient one.

To build this machine, let's start from the ground up, with a strong, solid base: feet shoulder-width apart, back slightly arched, butt sticking out, knees slightly flexed, and—most often overlooked—with the weight of your body on the inside of the balls of your feet. One of the most common affronts to the physics of the golf swing occurs when a player shifts his weight too far on the backswing, allowing his center of gravity to sway to the outside of his rear foot. From there, it's nearly impossible to shift your body weight forward on the downswing. Your body acts as a dead weight, pulling backward on the swing, leading to a weak, "casted" swipe. To avoid this fate, Arnold Palmer used to practice with golf balls stuck underneath the outside of his back foot, ensuring that his weight would remain on its instep.

The grip is the next great killer of potential energy, and almost always for one reason: Most golfers grip the club too tightly. Ben Crenshaw preaches that a golfer's grip pressure should be light enough to allow the club to feel "heavy" at the top of the backswing. Sam Snead said to imagine that you're holding a live bird in your hands; you might not want him to fly away, but—unless you're some kind of sick sadist—you don't want to hurt him, either. Let your bird breathe, and you'll allow your hands to transfer, as efficiently as possible, the potential energy from your body to the clubhead. To put it another way: Nobody cracks a whip with a stiff wrist.

You can't, of course, stand there like a statue on the first tee box forever. Eventually—despite the fear of abject humiliation—you must start your backswing. And when doing so, visualize what Nick Faldo refers to as the "coiling of the spring" of the torso. While your lower body remains stable and motionless, your shoulders should turn a full 90 degrees, creating tension, or torque, between the upper and lower body. Your backswing should also be as wide as possible; aim for the sensation of reaching straight back with the club, as if trying to hand it to someone far behind you—someone who's too lazy to come and get it. The wider the arc of the swing, the greater potential clubhead velocity, as, of course, distance/time = speed.

The downswing is best thought of as a simple uncoiling of your spring, an unfolding that starts at the feet: the lower body initiates the swing, with a shift of your weight from back foot to front, initiated by the rear knee "chasing" after the front knee, causing the hips to whip around to the target, thereby rotating the torso, which pulls the shoulders around, which, in turn, drag the hands along for the ride. Allow your hands to "drop" into the swing, retaining the hinge in the wrists that you set at the top of the backswing until you release your hands at the bottom of the swing. Think of your club as the helpless last kid of a "human whip" at the roller rink—being slung along by a sum of forces far greater than any one part.

As for the follow-through? Irrelevant. In truth, a golfer could release the club from his hands the moment after impact and it would make no difference—except, of course, to your playing partners, who might not appreciate having your eight-iron embedded between their shoulder blades. Still, a full release of your arms and torso, leading to a classic pose, with your belly button pointed to the target and your hands high above your front ear? Well, that always looks nice for the cameras.

THE WOODS SWING

Golfers appear to be the most stationary of athletes, but what separates Tiger Woods, the dominant golfer of modern times, from the rest of the pack is his speed.

No, we're not talking about how quickly he gets from one hole to another. The key to Tiger Woods's success is the tremendous speed of his swing, with recorded clubhead speeds at upwards of 130 mph, and ball speeds that approach 200 mph off his driver.

And what's fascinating about Tiger is that he's now been able to achieve those speeds with three different swings—and two totally different body types.

When he first burst onto the golf scene in 1996, Tiger was a whip-thin prodigy (6-foot-1 and 155 pounds) who generated his enormous distances through both an outrageously supple and forceful unwinding of his torso and a fairly radical "de-lofting" of his clubs at impact. At the time, Tiger would flatten his left wrist at impact, turning his five-iron, in essence, into a four-iron, and also reducing the spin on the ball, resulting in laser-like, flat-trajectory swings and balls that flew inconceivable distances (much farther than he hits it now). The problem: As an inevitable result of this, he had little idea where, or how far, his ball would fly.

After decimating the field in the 1997 Masters with this swing (the result of what Tiger would call a perfect week of rhythm and timing in his swing), he set out to rebuild it with the aid of Butch Harmon—shortening it, tightening it, making it more upright, and, most importantly, trying to eliminate his longtime tendency to get the club "stuck" behind him, a swing flaw that resulted in wild misses to the right of the fairway. This rebuilt swing produced the run of golf from 1999 to 2003 that was as dominant as any in the history of the game.

Unfortunately, it was unsustainable. The golf swing is a violent act, and Tiger's had begun to produce debilitating wear on his left knee. One result of his upright swing was that he would often hyperextend his left knee at impact, stressing several of the tendons. Forced to change after undergoing a second surgery on the knee in 2003, he sought the counsel of Hank Haney, who advocates a swing theory in almost diametric opposition to what Harmon had been teaching Tiger. Haney believes in a flat one-plane swing, which eliminates—in theory—much of the extraneous body action that was plaguing Woods. After a year or two of, essentially, reteaching

himself to swing the club, Tiger emerged as a dominant force again, winning five of twelve majors from 2004 to 2007, with more than twenty worldwide wins. Woods turned 35 years of age in 2010, the year he hired Sean Foley. Woods had been struggling with injuries and problems away from the course. Foley teaches a "stack and tilt" swing technique which in simpler terms focuses on the golfer keeping his weight centered, emphasizing balance throughout the swing. This balanced swing was attractive to Woods in that it reduced pressure on the knees that had caused him pain and frustration in the past.

DRIVERS AT SPEED

Clubhead speed for the average golfer with an iron is more than 80 mph when it hits the ball. With a driver, it nears 100 mph (with a ceiling of 125–130 mph for the longest-hitting pros). The club maintains contact with the ball for only one millisecond and exerts a force of 660 pounds. Initial ball speed off a driver is, for most pros, about 150 mph—upwards of 180 mph for such kinesiological freaks as Tiger Woods and John Daly.

NEW BALLS FALL SHORT

by DAVID GOULD

Augusta National Golf Club is fond of tradition, but renovating its golf course to accommodate increasingly longer drives is a practice the club has wearied of. The course has seen a 6.6 percent yardage increase over seven years (7,445 yards for the 2006 Masters Tournament compared to 6,985 in 1999)—the equivalent of one hole. That's led the influential club to join course architects and others in a push for new equipment regulations.

The U.S. Golf Association is listening and, in a first for the sports world, equipment manufacturers are being asked to make their products worse. Golf-ball makers have been told to submit prototypes that fly 15 to 25 yards shorter than current balls when driven at 120 mph. Reducing yardage will invariably mean rolling back technological advances that, over the past decade, have made the modern golf ball do its job so well. Too well, in fact.

1 Advance: Polybutadiene-based core boosts velocity for drives.

Rollback: "Unlink" the molecular structure for less efficient energy transfer.

2 Advance: Mantle increases acceleration and regulates spin.

Rollback: Soften the mantle so the ball regains its round shape less quickly.

3 Advance: Refined dimple shapes and geometry reduce drag.

Rollback: Revert to prior dimple configurations, increasing drag.

2006: 450 YARDS

1999: 365 YARDS

▲ Longer drives have led Augusta to add 85 yards to the seventh hole.

ARNOLD PALMER TALKS GOLF WITH PM IN 1964 AND 2011

by HARRY SAWYERS

This article appeared in POPULAR MECHANICS in 2011.

AT A CALLAWAY
EVENT IN NEW YORK,
THE KING MEETS
POPULAR MECHANICS
IN A TESTY, OVERDUE
REUNION.
ARNOLD PALMER
WAS SITTING
NEAR A TABLE OF
CRACKERS AND DIP
AT A CALLAWAY
GOLF PRESS EVENT
WHEN I APPROACHED
HIM. POPULAR
MECHANICS, I
EXPLAINED, HAD
COME DOWN TO THE
PRODUCT LAUNCH
TO TAKE A LOOK AT
THE LATEST IN GOLF
CLUB DESIGN AND
TECHNOLOGY.

"You did that already," Palmer said. "Must have been 1963 or 1964. I was in there testing what was considered the new technology at the time—steel shafts—against the old hickory types."

"Is that right?" I asked, jotting the dates in a notebook. "You wouldn't happen to know what issue that was in, would you?"

"I don't know, it was a long time ago," Palmer said. "You weren't even born yet!"

As it turns out, he was right. It was the July 1964 issue of PM. Palmer was always a tinkerer, adjusting his clubs and creating new ones, and so the magazine asked him to play a round with hickory-shaft clubs from 30 years prior to see just how much better the modern steel-shafted clubs of the 1960s performed. The King looked annoyed that I, an editor of *Popular Mechanics*, did not know that he'd graced our pages. He shook his head. "Back then, you know, some men even took their hats off indoors."

"Yes, Mr. Palmer!" I immediately reached to remove my tweed cap. Palmer guffawed upon seeing my bald head. "I see why you didn't take it off!" He laughed so heartily that his lustrous 82-year-old hair sort of vibrated.

(It must be stated that, riding New York's A train downtown to the event, I had written in my notebook "I hope Arnold Palmer likes my caddy hat." It was apparent that he did not.)

Clearly losing this round to the King, I explained, "If my dad were here, he'd have already told me to take the hat off."

"Oh yeah? Where are you from?" Palmer asked.

"Georgia," I replied.

"I've got some friends down in Georgia," said Palmer. No kidding: He won the Masters Tournament at Georgia's Augusta National Golf Club in 1958, 1960, 1962, and 1964. "Say hello to my people in Georgia, will ya?"

I agreed, and Palmer was summoned to the next room to give a speech about a familiar subject—advances in golf club technology. He spoke a few words on Callaway's new Razr Fit Driver, a $400 club with a forged composite crown and an adjustable face angle. The face's three positions, along with adjustable clubhead weights, can be used to correct a player's slice or hook. Palmer's talk is reminiscent of what he'd said in PM in '64: that the old-time hickory clubs offered too much room for error, especially for the non-pro. "What would feel like a good shot during the downstroke and at the moment of impact could well be a bad slice or a yardage-gaining hook, but he'd never be sure what caused the difference," he wrote then.

Palmer then recalled the time spent customizing clubs in his own shop, working with a hacksaw to shape their faces, and using a rasp to modify the tools further.

"I knew that if I could put together the perfect club, I could just put the ball right where I wanted it," he said. His statement could have been quoted from the story that Palmer and PM produced for our July 1964 issue—one that I'll now never forget.

A BRIEF HISTORY OF THE GOLF CLUB

by AMANDA GREEN

From blunt wooden instruments of the old days to today's adjustable, insanely high-tech drivers, golf clubs have been getting better and better since the Scots gave us this frustrating, exhilarating pastime.

960–1279: Royals from China's Song Dynasty play *chuiwan*, hitting balls into holes with a set of 10 bejeweled clubs.

1400s: Despite earlier evidence of proto-golf in the Netherlands, Scotland gets credit for inventing the game.

1800s: Par for the course, golf makes its way to the United States. Players use 20 to 30 wooden clubs of various functions to hit featheries, hard leather balls stuffed with feathers.

1856: America's hickory trees get the shaft when Robert Forgan exports them to Scotland to make golf clubs. Harder persimmon wood is used for the club heads until drop forging allows for mass-produced iron heads in the late 1800s.

1931: Billy Burke becomes the first golfer to win the U.S. Open using steel-shafted clubs painted to look like wood. But there's no faking Burke's unique grip—he only had three fingers on his left hand.

1932: Pro golfer Gene Sarazen thinks outside the sandbox to develop the modern sand wedge, and uses it in his British Open victory.

1939: Golf's rule-making authority decrees the use of no more than 14 clubs in a round but puts no limits on dorky apparel.

1959: Engineer Karsten Solheim invents a putter with more weight at the heel and toe of the blade and a thinner, lighter sweet spot. The novel design makes it easier for golfers to hit the ball straight. He quits his day job, creates the golf-equipment brand Ping, and makes a fortune.

1971: Alan Shepard takes one small swing for a man, one giant drive for mankind when he hits two golf balls on the moon at the end of the Apollo 14 mission. The second travels over a mile.

1973: Lightweight graphite-shaft clubs become popular among women and senior golfers. The rest of the world—ahem, PGA Tour players—catches on by the mid-1990s.

1980: In *Caddyshack*, Rodney Dangerfield's character stocks his bag with a driver that dispenses beer.

1991: Callaway rocks the golf world when it introduces the Big Bertha stainless-steel-headed driver. Persimmon-headed clubs quickly become garage-cluttering relics.

2013: TaylorMade's R1 driver adjusts to 12 different lofts and seven different face angles, adapting the club to playing conditions. Isn't that cheating?

CHAPTER 9

Hockey

SKATE FASTER

by LAURA STAMM

HOCKEY IS ALL ABOUT SPEED. TO ACHIEVE IT, ONE MUST APPLY THE PRINCIPLES OF FORCE APPLICATION EXPLOSIVELY AND WITH PRECISE TIMING (POWER). WHILE RAPID LEG MOTION IS IMPORTANT, SO IS THE CORRECT AND POWERFUL USE OF THE BLADE EDGES, LEGS, AND BODY WEIGHT. TOO MANY PLAYERS ARE TAUGHT TO MOVE THEIR FEET FAST REGARDLESS OF WHETHER OR NOT THEY ARE FOLLOWING THE PRINCIPLES OF FORCE APPLICATION. THESE PLAYERS MOVE AS IF ON A TREADMILL, WORKING HARD BUT GOING NOWHERE.

Michael Grabner of the New York Islanders earned a Calder Memorial Trophy nomination for NHL rookie of the year in 2010.

I created the C-cut exercise in 1971, and it remains one of my signature drills to this day. I named the push a C-cut because in executing the push, the skate scribes a cut in the ice that is similar to the letter "C" or a semicircular arc. The C-cut push is used for both forward and backward skating moves. This exercise focuses on the first third of the push for the forward stride that involves the heel (the midsole and the toe constitute the other parts). When done properly, the drill helps you develop a powerful push that generates speed.

ADVANTAGES OF THE C-CUT

In executing the forward C-cut, first the pushing leg moves to the back, then it curves out to extend sideways, moves forward, and completes the C by curving back to its starting position beneath the midline of the body. The C-cut exercise incorporates important skating and training fundamentals including:

> using the inside edges to cut powerfully into the ice when pushing

> thrusting first to the back and then to the side rather than directly back

> training the body to experience a fully extended, straightened free leg and a maximum-effort thrust, rather than a partially extended, weaker push

> training the gliding and pushing legs to work independently (while the glide is straightforward on a well-bent knee, the push is semicircular and the leg extends fully at the completion of the push)

> using the heel to begin each push of the forward stride (The toe of the blade is not used in the C-cut push; you push only with the back of the blade.)

The forward C-cut forms an upside-down letter C. In other words, the push begins at the bottom of the C and ends at the top of the C. The backward C-cut is exactly the reverse. The forward C-cut is skated with both skates on the ice at all times. Here's the twelve-step program designed to rid you of slowness on the ice. The left leg is the initial pushing leg.

1. Glide forward on the flats of both skates, feet directly under your body. Keep your back straight.

2. Prepare to push with the left leg while gliding straight ahead on the flat of the right skate.

3. Keep your weight on the back half of the thrusting (left) skate.

4. Bend your knees and dig the inside edge of the left skate into the ice so the skate and knee form a 45-degree angle to the ice. Concentrate your body weight over the edge.

5. Pivot the left foot outward with toe facing out to the side so that your skates approximate a right angle. Heels will be together and toes will be apart. You are now prepared to execute a C-cut push.

6. Cut the letter C into the ice with the left skate by pushing to the back, then outward until the pushing leg is fully extended out to the side.

7. At the mid-point of the C-cut thrust, transfer your weight onto the right skate, which is gliding straight ahead on the flat of the blade.

8. Thrust powerfully and to full extension. Keep the thrusting skate on the ice after the thrust is completed. The knee of the gliding leg remains well bent even when the thrusting leg is fully extended.

9. After the leg reaches its full extension, re-pivot the left skate. The left toe should now face inward (pigeon-toed) toward the gliding skate. This step is necessary in order to return the skate to its starting

Tomi Kallio, No. 71 of Finland, executes the C-cut during warm-ups before the 2006 International Ice Hockey Federation World Championship qualifying game between Canada and Finland at Riga Arena in Riga, Latvia.

position under your body. During the return, the skate no longer cuts into the ice. It glides back into the center under the body.

10. Move the left leg forward and then inward to its starting position centered underneath your body.

11. After the return, your feet should be side-by-side and centered under your body.

12. After returning, the left skate becomes the new gliding skate. To push again, place your weight on the inside edge of the right skate and cut a reverse and upside-down letter C with your right leg. Pivot the right skate, toe outward, and push front to back, then out to the side in a full extension. Then re-pivot the right skate (pigeon-toed) and bring it forward and then inward to its starting position centered under your body weight.

Remember: the push is a C-cut, not a silent C. The skate must cut into the ice. You should hear it. The sound indicates that your weight is over the pushing skate with the inside edge gripping the ice strongly.

The C-cut differs from the forward stride motion in that while the C-cut ends on your heel, the forward stride ends on your toe. Nevertheless, C-cut drills will improve your forward glide and help you develop the ability to generate more power off the initial push, and that will translate into faster skating.

FOR GOALIES, IT'S THE EYES THAT MATTER

by FRANK VIZARD

A FAST GLOVE AND A QUICK STICK MAY MATTER LESS TO HOCKEY GOALIES THAN WHERE THEY FOCUS THEIR EYES IN THE MOMENTS BEFORE AN OPPOSING PLAYER TAKES A SHOT ON GOAL.

While it may sound obvious, having your eyes focused on the puck and the shooter's stick in the second before the shot means the goalie is more likely to make the save, according to researchers at the University of Calgary.

Researchers Derek Panchuk and Professor Joan Vickers call this the Quiet Eye phenomenon, noting that novice goaltenders tend to let their gaze wander while elite goaltenders remain focused on the puck and shooter's stick. Vickers describes the Quiet Eye phenomenon as the critical moment when the eyes must receive and the brain must process the last piece of visual information before performing a critical movement. Using wireless headgear, the researchers were able to track a goalie's eye, body, and object movement to within 16.67 milliseconds. How far away the shot was didn't seem to matter in terms of a goalie's ability to make the save, as long as the puck was in view a second before the shot.

The study measured the eye movement of college-level goalies facing accomplished shooters one-on-one in a non-game situation. The goalies stopped the puck about 75 percent of the time under these conditions. In games, elite hockey goalies average about a 90 percent save rate, although the quality of the shots taken varies considerably.

SIX DEGREES OF SEPARATION

A goalie concentrating on the game.

22 DEGREES F. Temperature of ice in a rink preferred by figure skaters who like "soft" ice for better landings on jumps.

16 DEGREES F. Temperature preferred by hockey players who like "fast" ice that allows for more speed.

HOW BIG IS
YOUR STICK?

by FRANK VIZARD

FOR MANY PLAYERS, THE SIZE OF THE CURVE IN THE BLADE MAY MEAN THE DIFFERENCE BETWEEN AN ORDINARY CAREER AND A STELLAR ONE.

When hockey legend Brett Hull, who scored 741 goals with the St. Louis Blues and other teams, confessed to *Sports Illustrated* magazine that he used an illegal stick for most of his career, the revelation created a only minor tempest. Why? Unlike a corked bat in baseball, for example, the benefit of an illegal stick with a more pronounced curve on the blade is harder to definitely gauge in hockey.

In 2006, the National Hockey League changed its rule on how much curve in a blade is allowed, upping the limit to three-quarters of an inch from a half-inch. Scorers like Alex Ovechkin of the Washington Capitals, who was just coming off a 52-goal season, salivated in anticipation of the effect a 50 percent increase in the curvature of the blade would have on their goal production. By the end of the 2006–7 season, the effect was negligible. Ovechkin actually finished with 46 goals, and there was no noticeable uptick in scoring throughout the league.

Cynics might suggest that this only means most players were already using illegal sticks, perhaps since the three-quarter-inch blade was legal at the international and Olympic levels. Hockey players are notoriously attached to their sticks. The rush to the stick rack at the ten-minute mark of many games seemed to suggest that players were switching from legal to illegal sticks before an opposing coach could invoke the illegal-stick rule, if the score was close and the switch might affect the outcome of the contest. And should a player be caught with an illegal stick, the rule violation is considered a minor penalty and the fine is $200. Hull calls the regulation a "stupid rule" put it in place to protect goalies when they weren't very well padded and lacked helmets.

So what advantage can a longer curve on the blade of a stick provide? According to Alain Heche, a physicist at Moncton University and author of *The Physics of Hockey*, a longer curve should not add to the velocity of a shot puck, as speed is more of a by-product of the force with which the puck is hit. What a longer curve does provide is more consistency, since the puck always leaves the stick at the same place. The longer curve also gives a player more control of the puck, making it both easier to carry the puck around defenders and to grab the puck with the tip of

Right wing Brett Hull, No. 16 of the Phoenix Coyotes, skates against the Mighty Ducks of Anaheim during their preseason game at Arrowhead Pond in Anaheim, California, in September 2005.

the blade and shoot upward in one motion. A longer curve also puts more spin on the puck, which gives the puck more stability, making it that much more likely that the puck will go where a player is aiming. The reason for the curvature rule, notes Heche, is probably to limit puck control. In any event, any added benefit would be difficult to measure or even detect, he adds.

For many players, the size of the curve in the blade may mean the difference between an ordinary career and a stellar one. Brett Hull said he couldn't shoot without the curve on his stick. The question now is whether blades longer than three-quarters of an inch will appear, perhaps even approaching the banana-sized proportions used by Brett's father, Hall-of-Famer Bobby Hull. So keep an eye on the stick rack as the game winds down, when some players might switch to their illegal sticks. The team that risks playing with the most illegal sticks could have a deciding advantage.

PUCK SCIENCE

MATERIAL: Vulcanized rubber.

COLOR: Black.

SIZE: three inches in diameter, one inch thick.

WEIGHT: 5.5 to 5.6 ounces.

EDGE: Series of grooves or bumps so a taped hockey stick has something to grip on contact.

STORAGE: In freezers during a game to reduce bounce.

ORIGIN OF NAME: Unknown, but some suggest the name comes from the character of the same name in Shakespeare's *A Midsummer Night's Dream* as both move quickly and often in unexpected directions.

DATE OF INVENTION: The first puck was allegedly made around 1875 when Boston University students cut a rubber ball in half for use in a game.

BEST TV MOMENT: The 1995–96 NHL season when the Fox television network embedded a computer chip and cut twenty pinholes in the puck so that sensors could track it around the ice and viewers could find it more easily. At high speeds, the pucks developed a halo effect. Players complained that the puck didn't perform as well as the original. The idea was dropped.

DISTANCE A PUCK WILL TRAVEL ON ICE: If unimpeded by the rink, a puck shot at a speed of 100 mph—typical for a slap shot—would travel almost 1.2 miles (1.9 km) in 2 minutes 15 seconds, according to Professor Alain Heche of Moncton University in Canada.

WHY GRETZKY IS THE GREATEST

In a 1997 magazine interview, former St. Louis Blues goalie Mike Liut boiled the skill set of Wayne Gretzky, perhaps the greatest hockey player ever, down to a single question: "What don't I see that Wayne's seeing right now?"

By his own admission, Gretzky, who played most famously with the Edmonton Oilers as well as several other teams during the 1980s and 1990s, was not the strongest or fastest or most agile player on the ice even though he was named MVP of the National Hockey League nine times. What Gretzky did have was an ability that amounted to being able to see into the future and visualize what was going to happen in the next few seconds. In an article appearing in *Wired* magazine, scientists working for the U.S. Olympic team and the Australian Institute of Sport concluded that skills like Gretzky's come from an innate ability to intuitively translate physical cues dropped by opponents that are not apparent to most other athletes. Scientists are at work figuring out how this skill can be taught, but this type of perceptual training is still in its infancy. On the other hand, Gretzky may have just been following his father's advice, given to him when he was a youngster: "Skate to where the puck is going to be, not where it has been."

◀ All-Star Wayne Gretzky, active between 1978 and 1999, was said to have a magic touch with the puck, an accolade that stemmed from his great vision and mobility on the ice.

CONCUSSIONS IN HOCKEY

After Wayne Gretzky's retirement, hockey was in search of a new superstar and Sidney Crosby answered the call. The 5-11, 200-pound center joined the Pittsburgh Penguins in 2005-06, transforming the Penguins from the league's worst team to Stanley Cup champions by 2009. He famously scored the winning goal in overtime for Team Canada against the USA in the thrilling 2010 Winter Olympics gold-medal hockey game. However, Crosby's career was put in serious jeopardy with head injuries that took place in consecutive games played four days apart early in 2011. After returning home to Pittsburgh from the team's road trip to receive medical tests, the Penguins announced he would miss a week from a concussion. Crosby then announced that he would not return to the ice until the symptoms from his injury were gone and he suggested that the NHL should do more to punish and prevent blindside hits. Crosby's symptoms did not improve and he would not return for the rest of the season and missed a majority of the next season as well. The hits on Crosby sparked a rule change by the NHL stating that "players will now face a minor penalty for any hit that involves primary contact to the head and shots that target an opponent's head and make it the principal point of contact." This ruling was enacted to prevent hits to the head and prevent serious injuries from derailing player's careers. Crosby is just one of the latest hockey superstars who has had a concussion impact his career. Eric Lindros was once one of the most feared scorers in the NHL. He was the first overall pick in the 1991 draft and was traded to the Flyers soon after where he was selected to six All-Star games and was the MVP of the 1994-95 season. Lindros suffered a severe concussion following a hit to the jaw by New Jersey Devils defenseman Scott Stevens during the 2000 playoffs. The Flyers not only went on to lose that series, but also lost Lindros for the following season due to his concussion. Lindros was later traded to the New York Rangers and his career was never the same as he was no longer the powerful, dominating force that he once was. Crosby has been able to regain his form following his concussion, leading Pittsburgh to the Stanley Cup Finals in 2013.

CHAPTER 10

Running

MARATHON RUNNING

by DR. JOE VIGIL

DR. JOE VIGIL IS A LEGEND IN THE WORLD OF MARATHON RUNNING AND HAS BEEN LAUDED AS A "COACH SCIENTIST" FOR HIS ABILITY TO COMBINE SCIENCE AND ATHLETIC TRAINING DURING HIS 30-YEAR CAREER. VIGIL COACHED DEENA KASTOR TO A MARATHON BRONZE MEDAL AT THE 2004 OLYMPIC GAMES IN ATHENS, GREECE, CAPPING AN OLYMPIC TEAM ASSOCIATION DATING TO 1968. HERE, VIGIL, WHO BELIEVES DISTANCE RUNNING IS ENJOYING A RENAISSANCE, BREAKS DOWN A MARATHON.

Deena Kastor of the United States runs through the tape to win the women's 26th London Marathon on the Mall in front of Buckingham Palace on April 23, 2006. Kastor's time was 2:19:36.

PRIOR TO THE START

I pay attention to what a runner drinks 30 minutes before the start. You want to make sure the runner has enough liquids. I pre-determine how many ounces a runner should drink based on his or her size. We mix two powders, Accelerate and Endurox, with liquid. The mixture is four parts carbohydrate and one part protein. I make sure a runner is well hydrated and well fueled. If the race is early in the morning, a runner might eat a piece of toast or a bagel with jelly two or three hours before the marathon. You don't run the marathon on what you eat that day. You run on the fuel reserves you have built up from the previous days.

AT THE STARTING LINE

When a runner goes to the starting line, he or she already knows the course and the competition. Runners know what pace they are going to have to maintain. Olympic medalist Deena Kastor, for example, has a pre-determined pace that she is going to maintain. She knows how she feels at that pace because she has done it so many times in training. We determine that several different ways. I like to put her on a treadmill and determine her velocity at a respiratory quotient (RQ) of .94. That is the point at which she is burning pure fat more or less. This number can vary a hundredth of a percent from day to day because your metabolism varies from day to day as well. I've used .94 because it is a pretty good figure that you can rely on. In Deena's case, her velocity was 5 minutes 20 seconds per mile burning pure fat. That's what marathoners try to do. They try to utilize the energy derived from fat for the majority of the marathon. Everyone is different, though, in that runners will reach their .94 RQ at a different velocity. With Deena, her RQ velocity might go up or down a second on any given day depending upon her metabolism and the enzymes she has available. That's why you want to establish some constancy in the athlete in his or her eating and resting habits, so that it is about the same all the time. You have to live the lifestyle. The more variables you can control, the more predictable the result, just like any scientific experiment.

Geoffrey Mutai of Kenya ran the fastest recorded marathon on April 18, 2011, at the Boston Marathon. He finished the course in just 2 hours, 3 minutes, and 2 seconds (a 4:42 per mile pace).

THE FIRST FEW MILES

The first couple of miles, you have a great number of runners to contend with and there is a lot of nervous energy at play. You're trying to get away from the starting point to avoid injury and to prevent anyone from running into you. So sometimes you have to run a little faster than you would like that first mile to make space between you and the people behind you. If you're going to run in the lead group, you want to position yourself to be in contact with them.

Once you have good position, you settle down to your race pace. But here again, you're not always able to maintain a race pace if you have undulating terrain or if you have to run uphill or if the roar of the crowd is such that it motivates you—like the crowd coming off the 59th Street Bridge onto First Avenue in the New York Marathon. All runners experience a high when they hear people cheering. They can run a mile that is fifteen or twenty seconds faster than their race pace. You have to be careful. A marathon runner must always have emotional control over his or her pace. You can't be suckered into running someone else's race. That's why marathon runners should know themselves and the sensation of effort they are feeling at a particular pace. Once we've tested people and tell them what their relative pace might be, that's where we do the bulk of the training. Not all of it, because we challenge different energy systems. But since the marathon is a highly aerobic event, we spend 98 percent of our time within the aerobic range. If they do a hard aerobic run at marathon pace for 20 to 25 miles, the next day we'll schedule a low-intensity recovery run.

As the race progresses, we encounter other stresses. Is the wind blowing? Is it hot or humid? Is it raining or snowing? We then adjust our pace accordingly. When Deena ran the Olympic marathon in Athens, for example, it was 100 degrees at 6 p.m. and the newly laid asphalt was 120 degrees. When the men ran the marathon a week later, it was 85 degrees. The temperature determined how fast you could go because you had to endure the heat and the humidity for a longer period of time, and it takes more of an effort. Heat and humidity are the biggest stressors in the marathon. Deena started out relatively slowly. Because I had studied the past five Olympic marathons and the past six national championships, we knew what kind of time Deena had to run in order to medal.

Marathon runners are not as strong as sprinters. They don't have the muscle mass to produce the power to drive. The greater the force of the implant on the ground or track, the more driving force you get from the ground, especially on all-weather tracks that are so resilient they give energy back.

In a marathon, size works against you. Oxygen consumption is per kilogram of body weight. The bigger you are, the more calories you're going to burn. Efficient oxygen use, by the way, is very important. By slowly increasing her training runs to 100 to 110 miles per week, Deena gradually increased her VO2 MAX number—the amount of oxygen your body can use in one minute per kilogram of body weight—from 70.2 milliliters to 81.3 milliliters, one of the highest figures ever recorded for an American female athlete.

When you consider a marathon lasts two hours plus, any strength marathoners can develop, any fluidity in their mechanics that will enhance their striding pattern so that they can cover more ground per stride, is what they should shoot for. If you ran a 28-minute, 10,000-meter race and you improved your stride length two-thousandths of an inch per stride—that's derived from strength and power—you can lower that 10,000-meter time to 26 minutes flat. The most efficient running is evenly paced running. But not everyone can run an even pace. You have to know your body well. After nine years of coaching Deena, I would say that she is now finally in tune with her body in terms of marathon running. It's not an overnight phenomenon.

RUNNING THE MIDDLE MILES

Every runner knows what time he or she is supposed to hit at each mile or kilometer marker. If you're hitting these markers and you're running an even pace but find yourself in 100th place, you can't worry about it because you're running to your capacity. If you're leading the field, it tends to have a synergistic effect in that you start thinking you're really good and you run a little faster. If you're struggling to maintain your pace and people are ahead of you, you start thinking negative thoughts and that works against you. The mind is very powerful, and your mental state throughout the race is a determining factor in how successful you're going to be.

Because Deena looked so good when she won a bronze in Athens, people asked why she didn't run faster sooner. It's because she had an eight-mile incline to contemplate in addition to the heat and the humidity. Many women dropped out of the race, including world-record holder Paula Radcliffe at the 30K mark. If Deena had come out fast, she might have encountered the same difficulty. Instead, she had a negative split—meaning she ran the second half of the race faster than the first. She ran the last five kilometers in 16:09, partly because it was downhill. It also helped that I had found a course in California just like the one in Athens, and she ran it seven times at altitude before we went to Athens. I believe in the three A's: attitude, aptitude, and altitude. If you don't train at altitude, you're not going to compete with the best in the world. Over the past 20 years, people who live at altitude or who train at altitude have won 95 percent of the medals. By living and training at altitude, athletes can increase their red blood cell mass, which in turn enhances the athlete's oxygen-carrying capability.

HITTING THE WALL

The wall is the point at which you have depleted your level of carbohydrates. If you run faster than your RQ pace for an extended period of time, you will start using glycogen instead of fat. Deena's RQ velocity was 5:20, and that's the point where she is burning pure fat. You use fat as your source of energy and save your carbohydrates for the end. If you don't properly train, you'll race too fast and you won't be running aerobically, so you'll use up your carbohydrates or glucose. Whenever you use up your glucose, you hit the wall. You train to push the wall somewhere past the finish line. That's why pace is important in the marathon. If you know yourself, you'll maintain that pace at which you're burning fat. In your training, you're trying to develop the fastest velocity possible at which you're burning fat.

You can't hit the wall early during the race. You have about 410 grams of carbohydrates or glucose in your body. Each gram yields 4 calories of energy, so your glucose concentration will contribute 1,600 calories toward the marathon effort. Each gram of fat in your body contributes 9 calories toward the marathon effort. So it only stands to reason you would use the energy from fat because you have twice the amount of energy available (nine grams per calorie). And your stored fats are available in sufficient quantities that you could run many marathons provided you ran slowly enough. You need to save the glucose for the end of the race.

The problem, however, is that marathon runners tend to be lean. Elite woman marathoners have a body fat of between 10 and 12 percent, while elite men are in the range of 4 to 8 percent. It's difficult to add body fat when you're training hard. But there is also a thing we call "critical fat," which is the percentage of fat that you have to maintain in order for normal metabolism, hormone and enzyme production, to take place. The critical point for women is 9 percent body fat and for men it is 3 percent. So you never want to go below that or you have to cut back on training. Ideally, a woman should stay above 10 percent and a man above 4 percent.

You can run a marathon on less than one pound of fat. One pound of fat yields 3,500 calories, and it normally takes about 2,700 to 2,800 calories for a man to run a marathon and 2,400 calories for a woman. So everyone has the energy to do it, but the pace is the regulator of how that energy is going to be used. You have to have emotional control during the race or you won't have the energy to finish it. You have to know a little something about your body and what it is capable of. That's the hard part with coaching.

THE LAST FEW MILES

The race doesn't really begin until the last five or six miles. What happens now is that runners start surging, testing one another. One runner will surge to see who will stay with him or her. At a given point, they will break into a fast mile of about 4:30. With a surge you are trying to upset a competitor's pace, but you run the risk of ruining your own. So you practice surging, asking runners to run faster than race pace the last two or three miles of a tempo run. But at this point in the competition, a lot of runners will be running beyond their capacity. Surges will narrow the field because some runners are forced to dip into their carbohydrate bank for additional energy.

If there are runners bunched together with 400 meters to go, then the marathon becomes a sprint. This is where the carbohydrates or glucose is expended. This is where runners tap into different energy sources called the alactate and lactate systems to sprint the last few yards if need be. At this point, it is a question of who can hang on to win. The biggest excitement for me is that I know what it takes to achieve those world-class times. I've developed a lot of respect for those athletes who can stick to a regimen and produce those results.

TALKING SHOE

What's the future of the running shoe? How about a shoe that talks to you? A running shoe from Nike is able to send data wirelessly to Apple's portable iPod music player, allowing a runner to monitor his performance while listening to downloaded coaching advice. Runners also will be able to upload their personal stats onto a Nike website and compare them with others. Where Nike leads, others are sure to follow.

The Nike + iPod Sport Kit is basically a small oval pod that fits under the liner of the running shoe. It looks much like a SIM card used in a cellphone, and it transmits a variety of data such as time and distance to a receiver that connects to your iPod. Apple also offers special workout music mixes that can be downloaded to the iPod so that inspirational music can get you past the next milestone.

CHIPS FOR SHOES

The future of running shoes may have already arrived in the form of a running shoe that uses a computer to adjust itself during the course of the run. The Adidas_1 Intelligence Level 1.1 is equipped with a small sensor and a magnet that tells a tiny computer embedded in the shoe when the cushioning level is too soft or too firm. The sensor sits just below the runner's heel, and the magnet is placed at the bottom of the midsole. The system gauges the compression on impact and deduces the amount of cushioning being employed. About 1,000 readings per second are relayed to the computer located under the arch of the shoe. By comparing the incoming data against a preset model, the shoe can determine if the cushioning is too soft or too hard. The microprocessor then commands a motor-driven cable to either tighten or loosen a screw accordingly. The entire system runs off a small battery—so the next time you see a runner adjusting his shoe, he may not be tying his shoelaces but replacing a battery.

THE RUNNING SHOE DEBATE: HOW BAREFOOT RUNNERS ARE SHAPING THE SHOE INDUSTRY

by TYGHE TRIMBLE

This article appeared in POPULAR MECHANICS in 2009.

A GROUP OF RUNNING REBELS ARE SHEDDING THEIR SHOES AND REPORTING YEARS OF INJURY-FREE MILES. SOME ULTRAMARATHONERS, BIOMECHANICS EXPERTS AND DOCTORS THINK THAT'S PROBABLY A GOOD THING. OTHERS GO SO FAR AS TO SAY RUNNING SHOES ARE IN FACT *CAUSING* INJURIES.

Aerial view of New York City Marathon runners crossing the Verrazano-Narrows Bridge near the start of the race on November 3, 1996.

Meanwhile, running shoe companies continue to precisely measure runners, and pound and flex shoes in their high-tech labs. Could shoes—and shoe companies—be covering hundreds of thousands of perfectly able bare feet? If shoes are doing damage, just what are the companies measuring?

The Boston Marathon, one of the world's most competitive 26.2-mile races, had the best runners from Kenya, Ethiopia, the U.S. and around the globe churning out 5-minute miles on Monday for over two hours. While all eyes were on the front-runners—notably the United States' Ryan Hall (third) and Kara Goucher (third among female racers)—way back in the pack there was one person, Rick Roeber, who stole headlines with his unique running style. One glance at Roeber's feet and you can see what all the fuss is about: he isn't wearing shoes. And a number of people—ultramarathoners, biomechanics experts and doctors included—think that's probably the best way to run. Some go so far as to say running shoes are in fact causing injuries.

While entry into the Boston Marathon is a feat in itself—Roeber needed to have about an 8-minute-mile pace over 26 miles to qualify—attempting the race barefoot is something most runners would find an absurd, even obscene, gesture. Runners are hooked on shoes. For good reason, it would appear: Ranging from 5 mm to 22 mm thick and made mostly of polymer, running shoes are engineered to support feet for mile after mile of rough asphalt and rocky terrain. They protect vulnerable soles from glass and debris, provide padding and, shoe companies claim, help correct problematic twists and turns of our ankles and legs caused by excessive pronation.

But to barefoot advocates such as Chris McDougall, author of *Born to Run* (Knopf), Roeber is one of the few in Monday's race not drinking the shoe industry's Kool-Aid. In his book, McDougall follows the Tarahumara, a Mexican tribe of ultrarunners who race from 50 to 200 miles straight without shoes, yet remain healthy and injury-free. Science doesn't support the shoe industry's claim that "humans are born broken," McDougall tells PM, and that running shoes exist to fix our stride. Humans have been barefoot for nearly 2 million years, but have had running shoes for only a little more than 40—when Nike-founder Bill Bowerman cobbled together the modern-day running shoe with glues, plastic and a waffle iron in his basement. Shoes cause runners to lose musculature in their feet, McDougall argues, and takes away the natural cushion in their stride.

Could shoes—and shoe companies—be part of a $25 billion snake oil industry, covering hundreds of thousands of perfectly able bare feet? Or is barefoot running dangerous for marathoners and weekend joggers alike? That's the debate now brewing in the running community. The answer depends in part on a classic chicken and egg question: Do we run the way we do because of running shoes, or do running shoes support the way we now run?

TAKING IT IN STRIDE

In a back room at the $2 million New Balance running shoe research and development lab in Lawrence, Mass., the MTS 858 Mini Bionix II—a giant hydraulic piston with the cast of a foot attached—loudly pounds into the heel of a light blue, cushioned running shoe. This stress-testing machine, made by the same company that builds earthquake simulators, can apply 5,620 pounds of force to a shoe 30 times every second (although researchers at New Balance tend to be gentler on the footwear). Down the hall, a glass plate sitting in the middle of a polished wooden floor conceals a camera that measures the impact of the shoe on the ground. Cameras also capture the light reflected by tiny silver dots worn by a runner on a treadmill, tracking hundreds of points on the body during each stride. Across the room, an outline of feet projected onto the wall conveys the treadmill runner's footstrike in real time. Meanwhile, a computer records streams of data relaying angle and force, to be interpreted and analyzed by researchers later. This is high-tech biomechanics, all in the service of designing the perfect running shoe.

Some researchers and runners think this ideal shoe will be cushioned and wide, with high-tech gels, plastics and perhaps even moving parts to better absorb shock. To others, the perfect shoe looks more like a sock, with only a thin cover to protect feet from glass and other ground hazards. The two design camps split cleanly between catering to different strides: While the barefoot runner's gait tends to strike on the forefoot, a significant amount of shoe technology is aimed toward a heel-to-toe motion. A study from 1980, which was repeatedly cited by shoe experts at the New Balance labs, reveals how much more prevalent heel-to-toe running is. Analyzing the form of 753 runners, biomechanical researcher Benno Nigg found that 80 percent of runners (videotaped in two races) ran with a heel-to-toe motion; 45 percent of the faster runners (those with a 5-minute, 18-second-mile pace or better) ran heel-to-toe-step; the rest ran with what he calls a midfoot strike, in which the heel and forefoot strike the ground simultaneously.

THE MORE PERFECT SHOE

With or without shoes, humans are evolved to run. In a 2004 study published in *Nature*, Dennis Bramble and Daniel Lieberman provide clear physiological evidence of this: Humans are efficient sweaters, for one. We also have tall bodies with ample surface area to cool ourselves, large buttocks with muscles critical for stabilization in running, and long legs that include Achilles tendons—ideal for storing and releasing mechanical energy. These features, the authors argue, allowed us to be superior scavengers and even hunters (by tracking sprinting animals).

The problem modern-day runners face, according to Hugh Herr, Popular Mechanics 2005 Breakthrough Award winner and head of the biomechatronic group at MIT, isn't presented by our bodies but by the evolution of running surfaces. Humans that ran to scavenge or hunt for their food weren't pounding concrete. Herr is in a unique position to weigh in on shoe technology. He defended the double-prosthetic sprinter, Oscar Pistorius, in his appeal to the International Association of Athletics Federations board last year against charges that his Cheetah prosthetics provided a mechanical advantage. Herr also invented the iWalk Powerfoot One, the most advanced robotic ankle in existence.

Bare feet just aren't meant to support running on modern day hard-top surfaces, Herr says. In his research, Herr focused on two problems with both shod and barefoot running-pronation angle and impact force. While barefoot running is best for a natural, stress-free pronation angle, Herr says, it is not ideal for coping with roads and sidewalks that can lead to stress-impact injuries. Shoes, on the other hand, excel at diminishing the force of impact on hard ground. But they do so at the cost of the natural stride-all the padding added to the shoe exaggerates the foot's rotation. "It's hard to design a shoe with pronation as small as what exists naturally," Herr says. "When you're barefoot, you have the advantage of the heel being very thin [and thus diminishing rotation]."

Herr's solution to the problem of shoe design is to start from scratch and fundamentally redesign the running shoe. His first-stage prototype looks nothing like any shoe for sale today. Called the SpringBuck, Herr's shoe is form fitting, taking advantage of the barefoot runner's naturally low pronation, while a spring-like heel diminishes the impact of feet on hard surfaces. This shoe even shows a metabolic reduction for the runner, Herr says, thanks to the optimized stride. Though no doubt radical to barefoot advocates and shoe labs alike, a running shoe that rethinks humans' relationship with their environment may fill the vacuum of science on the great shoe debate, and finally provide a one-size-fits-all solution.

PICK THE RIGHT SHOE

Picking the right running shoe depends upon the type of foot you have. Foot types can basically be lumped into three categories: normal, flat, and arched. Match the right shoe to the right foot type and you'll avoid a lot of pain.

So which type of foot do you have? Find out by wetting a pair of brown bags and then standing on them in your bare feet. The resulting imprint will tell you a lot.

If the heel and the ball of the footprint are connected and there is a slight indentation where the arch is, then you have normal feet. When running,

a normal foot generally lands on the outside of the heel with a slight inward roll on each stride. All the foot needs is a little stabilization, so look for a shoe with a firm sole and a slight curve on the bottom.

Flat feet that have little or no arch tend to roll too far inward. This puts too much of the body's weight on the inner sole and, in time, may lead to pain in the ankles and hips. A shoe that compensates for this pronation should have a very stiff midsole to keep the foot from rolling too far inward.

By contrast, feet with

high arches require a shoe flexible enough to let the foot roll inward more. Otherwise, high arches can cause feet to roll over on their edges. A well-cushioned, slightly curved running shoe usually corrects the problem.

Like a car that needs to change its tires after a number of miles, you should expect to change running shoes every 300 to 500 miles. If you feel a twinge in your legs where there was none before, or fatigue in your hips and knees, it may be an early sign that your running shoe needs replacement.

Skiing

SPEED SKIING

by CHARLES
PLUEDDEMAN

SPEED SKIING, THE PURSUIT OF PEAK VELOCITY, IS THE MOST INTENSE AND THRILLING OF ALL THE SKIING DISCIPLINES. WIND TEARS AT YOUR BODY AND THE SKIS FLOP AS YOU FIGHT TO HOLD A TUCK POSITION. AS YOU HURTLE DOWN THE COURSE, PASSING THROUGH TIMING LIGHTS, YOUR BODY PUNCHES A HOLE IN THE ATMOSPHERE THAT RIPS THE AIR WITH A JET-ENGINE ROAR. SLOWING DOWN IN THE BRAKING AREA, YOU GLANCE AT THE SCOREBOARD TO SEE YOUR SPEED CLOCKED IN EXCESS OF 140 MPH. ANY FASTER AND YOU'D NEED A PARACHUTE.

◀ Sanna Tidstrand of Sweden competes on her way to capturing the women's Gold Medal at the FIS Speed Skiing World Championships in Verbier, Switzerland, in April 2007.

THE HISTORY OF SPEED SKIING

The origin of speed skiing dates to 1898, when a Californian, Tommy Todd, allegedly zipped to 87 mph (about 139 kph). However, the first official record was set in 1932, when Italian skier Leo Gasperi was clocked at 89 mph (about 142 kph) by the International Ski Federation / Fédération Internationale de Ski (FIS) in St. Moritz, Switzerland. By the 1960s, speed skiing was a professional sport sanctioned by the FIS. It was also accorded the status of a demonstration sport in the 1992 Winter Olympics in Albertville, France.

SPECIALIZED EQUIPMENT

The basic goal of speed skiing is to harness gravity and defeat friction. To this end, the equipment is highly specialized. The skis are about 240 centimeters long, compared to 225 centimeters for a downhill racing ski and 200 centimeters for a recreational ski. In addition, the skis are 10 centimeters wide and made of wood and steel, which contributes to their hefty 25-pound weight.

The extra width helps the skis run flat on the snow and spread out the skier's weight over the largest possible area to reduce friction. To keep the tips on the snow at speeds over 100 mph, the skis are rigid, heavily damped, and shaped to cut a low profile for minimal wind resistance.

While speed skiers use widely available high-performance bindings and boots, they typically fit the bindings with a stiff racing spring and modify the boot cuffs to provide a sharp forward lean in the lower leg, which allows the racer to bend low in the tuck position.

To help air pass smoothly over their bodies, speed skiers squeeze into skintight suits. The suit's material is typically a stretch fabric that may be coated with polyurethane, for example, to give it density to resist the formation of slipstream bubbles in low-pressure zones along the racer's body. Each suit is custom-cut to fit the racer's body.

To smooth the airflow around the lower legs, a wedge-shaped fairing made of dense foam fits inside the suit behind each calf from the knee to the boot top. Interestingly, airflow concerns also play a part in glove design. Speed skiers use their hands as the leading edge to break the wind and to act as a controlling rudder. The gloves, also made of a stretch material, have special cuffs that allow the air to flow smoothly over the wrists.

Speed skiers use poles to push off at the starting point and to act as a framework for bracing their arms next to their bodies. The poles are custom-bent to wrap around a skier's torso. Cones fitted to the end of each grip also help to streamline air.

According to U.S. speed skier Jeff Hamilton, the speed skier's helmet is his most essential piece of equipment. Hamilton should know. In 1995, he was ranked the fastest skier in the world, with a mark of 242 kph (150.4 mph) set in Vars, France.

"Each helmet is custom-made to fit the racer's body size and tuck position," explains Hamilton. "It directs wind from the top of the head in a straight line down the back. A slight change in the shape of the helmet can cause a one-mile-per-hour or more difference in top speed."

Hamilton's helmet was molded from a combination of Kevlar and fiberglass. Some helmets are designed with a fin along the top to increase stability and to allow the racer to steer by moving his head.

Another essential element is the preparation of the ski bases. Hamilton tuned his skis to fit conditions by using a stone grinder to create varied structural patterns and then applied one of several types of wax. There are only about ten speed-skiing courses in the world capable of hosting a World Cup–level event. Each course must be able to safely produce speeds of at least 170 kph (about 106 mph).

THE RACING COURSE

The racer's speed potential is dictated by the location of the starting point, which is typically 300 to 400 meters (984–1,312 feet) above the first timing light. Race officials determine the starting point after calculating snow and weather conditions, the steepness of the hill, and the ability of the athletes entered in the race. In an effort to promote safety, the FIS has mandated that a starting point must be chosen that will not produce a speed above

Two views of the speed skier's tuck. Boots are modified to provide a sharp forward lean. The head is lower than the butt so that airflow on the back produces downward pressure. Note the aerodynamic contours of the helmet.

228 kph (about 142 mph). The rule is intended to encourage athletes to compete for the fastest speed at each event, rather than just gunning for a new record. When a record is set, it is a true accomplishment.

Skiers study the course before each run and pick the smoothest path to the speed trap: two sets of timing lights set 100 meters (about 328 feet) apart. To start, the skier simply stands perpendicular to the fall line of the hill, picks his line, and then jumps to face downhill. From there, gravity and technique take over.

Since skiers reach top speed in less than 400 meters (1,312 feet), initial acceleration is critical. Ski tuning plays an important role here, as does the technique of keeping flat on the snow and maintaining an optimal tuck position: head low and butt high to create downward pressure. Initially, Hamilton holds his hands positioned in front of his helmet, but as he builds speed he gradually extends his arms out about eight inches in front of his body.

In less than fifteen seconds, acceleration goes from zero to more than 225 kph (140 mph). The entire run takes just twenty seconds, but it is a very intense twenty seconds with little margin for error.

A red line in the snow signals the end of the speed trap, and the skier begins the process of slowing down—the most dangerous part of the run. On slower courses, where speeds don't go much above 161 kph (100 mph), skiers can just stand up and use the wind as a brake. But at 225 kph (140 mph), you must slowly untuck to dirty the aerodynamics. Below 161 kph (100 mph), you can carve very wide turns to burn off speed.

For each round in a multi-day event, the starting point is moved higher up the hill. There are four to six rounds in a typical meet, and the fastest skier in the final round is declared the winner.

Defying the best efforts of the FIS, speed skiers continue to bump the world speed record upward at sanctioned meets. Is there a limit to speed on the snow?

For years, many skiers considered 250 kph (155.343 mph) a "mythical border," but in 2002 it was passed by Philippe Goitschel at Les Arcs, France, with a speed of 250.70 kph (155.778 mph). That record has since been broken by Simone Origone, who clocked in at 252.4 kph (156.834 mph) at Les Arcs in 2006.

▲ **Special equipment, from top:** A wedge-shaped fairing fits inside the stretch suit at the back of each calf, poles that wrap around the torso are used as a framework for bracing the arms in position, and aero gloves are used to break the wind and act as a partial rudder.

SKI JUMPING: IN-FLIGHT ADJUSTMENTS

by ALEX HUTCHINSON

IT'S WELL
ESTABLISHED THAT
A SKI JUMPER'S BODY
AND SKIS WORK LIKE
AN AIRPLANE WING.

They direct the onrushing wind downward, forcing the air rushing over the top of the body and skis to flow faster than the air below. In a demonstration of Bernoulli's principle, this creates lower pressure on the topside of the skier than below him, pulling him upward. But ski jumpers aren't just like airplane wings—they're like airplane wings with precise controls. Austrian researchers Bernhard Schmölzer and Wolfram Müller studied competitors at the 2002 Olympics, where the jumping was held in Park City, Utah, at an unusually high altitude of more than 6,500 feet. Top jumpers compensated for the decreased lift (and drag) of the thin air by adjusting the angle between their bodies and skis to an average of 16.1 degrees, greater than the 11.7 degrees seen at lower elevations. The 2006 Olympic ski-jumping events were held at 5,000 feet in the Italian town of Pragelato.

▶ In 2002, airfoil-like ski-jumping champion Simon Ammann flew 186 feet farther than if— like a cannonball—he'd experienced no lift.

◀ Ski jumpers such as champion Simon Ammann can widen the angle between their bodies and skis to gain lift.

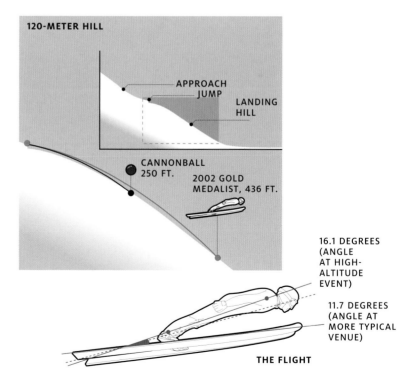

120-METER HILL

APPROACH
JUMP
LANDING
HILL

CANNONBALL
250 FT.

2002 GOLD
MEDALIST, 436 FT.

16.1 DEGREES
(ANGLE
AT HIGH-
ALTITUDE
EVENT)

11.7 DEGREES
(ANGLE AT
MORE TYPICAL
VENUE)

THE FLIGHT

SNOWBOARDING'S TWISTING FORCES

by ALEX HUTCHINSON

Olympic snowboarder Danny Kass is brilliant at improvising during his halfpipe runs, says U.S. Olympic coach Mike Jankowski. But some things are set the instant he launches from the lip of the eighteen-foot-high pipe. The path his center of mass will take—how high he soars and where he lands—is determined by his approach. And the angular momentum for the flips and rotations he does fifteen feet off the deck must be generated before he leaves the snow. Top riders can spin through 1440 degrees (four rotations), but more in the spirit of the sport are the back-to-back inverted 1080s that Kass pioneered—which use every trick in Isaac Newton's playbook.

Two-time Olympic gold medalist Shaun White holds the X-Games record for highest overall medal count. At Winter X, he became the first person to score a perfect 100 in the men's Snowboard Superpipe in the history of the games.

Soccer

BEND IT LIKE BECKHAM

by FRANK VIZARD

IF YOU'RE EVEN REMOTELY FAMILIAR WITH SOCCER, THEN YOU KNOW THAT THE PHRASE "BEND IT LIKE BECKHAM" HAS ENTERED THE SPORTS LEXICON AND EVEN APPEARED AS THE TITLE OF A POPULAR BRITISH FILM IN 2002. BECKHAM, OF COURSE, IS DAVID BECKHAM, THE FORMER SUPERSTAR OF ENGLISH SOCCER. BUT WHAT'S THIS "BEND IT" BUSINESS ALL ABOUT?

British soccer legend David Beckham.

THE INFAMOUS SHOT

It's October 6, 2001. England is playing Greece. A qualifying berth in the World Cup is on the line. In the waning seconds of the game, the English side is awarded a free kick. Beckham places the ball down on the pitch 27 meters (about 89 feet) from the goal, and a defensive wall of Greek players lines up between him and the goal. The tension is palpable. If you're a baseball fan and new to soccer, think bottom of the ninth, two outs, and the batter represents the winning run for a post-season appearance. What happened next has become the most scientifically analyzed kick in the history of soccer.

Beckham's shot left his foot traveling at about 80 mph with lots of spin on it. The ball soared over the defensive wall by a half meter (just under twenty inches). If the ball continued at this rate of speed and at the same trajectory, it would sail over the crossbar, dashing England's hopes. But just as it cleared the defensive wall, the ball moved laterally about three meters (just under ten feet) and then slowed to a speed of 42 mph as if making a mid-flight correction. To the astonishment of the Greek goalkeeper, the ball dipped into the corner of the goal. In little more than a second, England had qualified for the World Cup by riding Beckham's leg, and "Bend It Like Beckham" became a mantra.

STUDY OF THE BEND

What happened? Was Beckham some kind of magician? If so, he was not alone. In a 1997 tournament game in France, Brazilian Roberto Carlos took a free kick about 20 meters (about 66 feet) from the opposing goal. Carlos kicked the ball over the defensive wall, but so far to the right of the goal that a ball boy ducked his head in anticipation. But then the ball curved left and slipped into the top-right corner of the net to the amazement of everyone except Carlos, who frequently practiced the kick during training.

The Carlos kick inspired a 1998 article in *Physics World*, but the scientific community didn't get behind soccer until the Beckham kick, probably due to its sensational impact and the availability of high-quality video footage taken from multiple angles. Scientists at the University of Sheffield's Sports Engineering Research Group in England, Yamagata University's

Sports Science Laboratory in Japan, and Fluent, a maker of computational fluid dynamics software, joined forces to learn how to bend it like Beckham. Their goal was three-fold.

"I believe that it would now be possible to design an optimum free kick for any given point outside the penalty area and to train young players to reproduce these optimum kicks," said Dr. Keith Hanna of Fluent. The scientists also hoped their research would help ball manufacturers fine-tune the aerodynamics of soccer balls so they would be more responsive to the pace and spin applied by players. Lastly, they hoped their research would lead to the design of boots that imparted spin more effectively while reducing foot injuries.

SCIENCE BEHIND THE KICK

Soccer players know that if you kick the ball slightly off-center with the front of your foot while your ankle is bent like an "L," the ball will curve in flight. The curving flight plan combined with the reduction in speed of the soccer ball was perhaps less well understood, as the study of soccer balls in flight had not been analyzed as much as, say, golf balls and baseballs. But like these other types of balls, scientists knew that soccer balls are subject to a lateral deflection effect called the Magnus force. Gustav Magnus was a German scientist who, in 1852, determined why spinning bullets and shells deflect to one side. As it happens, his explanation also works well for balls.

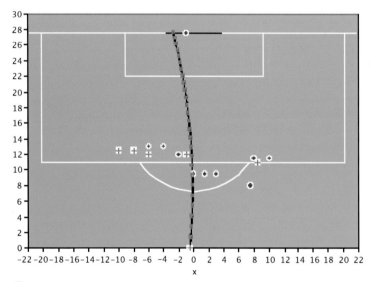

Graph shows the trajectory of Beckham's free kick versus Greece in the 2001 World Cup qualifier.

But the Magnus force didn't explain everything. Coupled with the Magnus force was a sudden transition in the airflow surrounding the ball as its speed decreased approaching the goal. During this shift between what scientists call a turbulent and a laminar flow, the amount of drag on the ball increased by 150 percent in a split second. This is what caused the ball to dip at the last moment. Just when this transition occurs varies with the rate of the spin on the ball and the type of surface seam pattern used on the ball. At a high spin rate, the transition occurs at faster ball speeds.

Somehow, through a combination of instinct, training, and practice, Beckham knew that this transition would occur once the ball had cleared the defensive wall of Greek players. Dr. Matt Carre of the University of Sheffield notes that "almost certainly the flow around the ball changed from turbulent to laminar several meters from the goal because otherwise our calculations suggest it would have gone over the crossbar."

Computational fluid dynamics analysis, in fact, recorded the airflow behind the ball changing with the speed of the ball, indicating that complex forces were affecting the flight path of the ball. Computer simulation also allowed scientists to deduce where the "sweet spot" of the ball was for creating maximum spin. That spot turned out to be 80 millimeters off-center, and when hit, ball spin was measured at eight revolutions per second. By contrast, kicking the ball at a spot 40 millimeters off-center reduced the rate of spin to four revolutions per second. A couple of degrees of variation in the direction of the kick or in the axis of the spin would have changed the outcome for England.

INFLUENCE OF THE BALL

Goalkeepers, meanwhile, are fooled by soccer balls that sometimes swerve in a S-shaped pattern even when the kicker puts no spin on the ball. The same group of researchers concluded after a battery of tests that the ball's panel design affected trajectory through the air. After examining balls used over a 36-year period, they discovered that drag on non-spinning balls had fallen as much as 30 percent as the balls became progressively smoother and rounder. In fact, the Adidas ball used in the 2010 World Cup had only eight bonded sections rather than the traditional 32-hand-stitched panels.

What all this means is that a talented soccer player can kick the ball, spin or no spin, with more precision than ever before. Combine new ball technology with a better understanding of the physics of ball movement, and you'll soon have players bending it like Beckham almost at will. Beckham, meanwhile, continued to bend the ball practically on demand, as his electrifying 23-meter (25-yard) goal to eliminate Ecuador 1–0 in the 2006 World Cup in Germany demonstrates, proving, once again, why he was the most dangerous man in the world off a set piece like a free kick.

FOLLOW THE
BOUNCING BALL

THE WORLD CUP, HELD EVERY FOUR YEARS, IS SOCCER'S GREATEST SHOWCASE. FOR FOUR DECADES, ADIDAS HAS SUPPLIED SOCCER BALLS FOR THE WORLD CUP, AND THIS RECORD PROVIDES INSIGHT INTO THE BALL'S EVOLUTION.

1970

The leather Telstar ball, with its twelve black pentagons and twenty white hexagons, featured 32 hand-stitched panels and became synonymous with soccer. The black pentagons were introduced because the 1970 World Cup in Mexico was the first to be televised and the new ball was more visible on black-and-white television. The ball made a repeat appearance in Germany in 1974.

1978

The Tango ball used in the Argentina World Cup is considered a design classic. Twenty panels with "triads" created an optical illusion of twelve identical circles. Balls used in the next five World Cup competitions were based on this design.

1982

The Tango ball in the World Cup in Spain used waterproof sealed seams for the first time. This reduced the ball's water absorption capabilities so the ball didn't get heavier during games played in wet conditions.

Portuguese forward Cristiano Ronaldo (right) controls the ball in front of Iranian defender Hossein Kaabi during the 2006 World Cup group D football game, Portugal vs. Iran, on June 17 at FIFA World Cup Stadium Frankfurt in Frankfurt am Main, Germany.

1 9 8 6

The Azteca model used in Mexico was the first synthetic ball used for a World Cup. It was lauded for its better performance on hard ground, in wet conditions, and at high altitude.

1 9 9 0

An internal layer of black polyurethane foam made the Etrusco Unico ball used in Italy livelier, faster, and more water-resistant. Three Etruscan lions decorated each of the twenty Tango triads.

1 9 9 4

A high-energy-return layer of white polyethylene made the Questra model used for the USA World Cup softer to the touch (and therefore more controllable), and it was much faster off the foot for more speed.

1 9 9 8

The first multi-colored Tricolore ball, used for the World Cup in France, featured a layer of gas-filled micro-balloons designed to improve the ball's energy return as well as its responsiveness and durability.

2 0 0 2

With a new exterior look for the World Cup games held jointly in South Korea and Japan, the Fevernova ball also added a three-layer, knitted chassis for a more precise and predictable flight path every time.

2 0 0 6

The +Teamgeist ball unveiled for the World Cup in Germany used a new thermal-bonded fourteen-panel construction that offered players an increased number of smoother surfaces for kicking in order to improve accuracy and control.

2 0 1 0

The Jabulani ball used for the World Cup in South Africa was created using a wind tunnel which resulted in a highly calibrated ball of optimal roundness and stable flight.

SAFE HEADERS?

by FRANK VIZARD

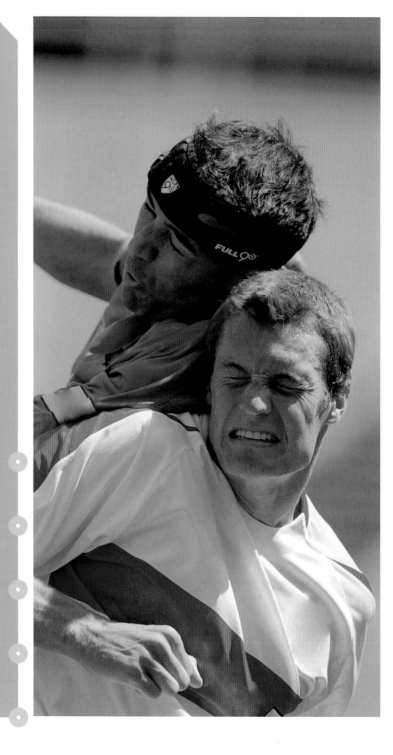

WE'VE ALL SEEN IT: A SOCCER PLAYER LEAPS INTO THE AIR AND REDIRECTS A KICKED BALL WITH HIS HEAD. IT'S ONE OF THE MOST THRILLING PLAYS IN SOCCER, AND A TEAM OF GOOD HEADERS IS SAID TO DOMINATE THE AIR. BUT IS HEAD-TO-BALL CONTACT SAFE? DOES IT LEAD TO CONCUSSIONS?

◀ Head-to-head contact, rather than head-to-ball, is more likely to result in a concussion, say scientists.

▼ Crash-test dummies are used to gauge collision impacts on all critical areas of the head.

The answer appears to be "no," according to the *British Journal of Sports Medicine* (*BJSM*), a peer-reviewed medical journal. Working with a Canadian laboratory and the International Federation of Association Football (FIFA), soccer's governing body, *BJSM* concluded that the forces associated with head-to-ball contact are not strong enough to cause a concussion. The lab, Biokinetics & Associates Ltd. of Ottawa, Ontario, examined video showing 62 cases of head impact on the soccer field and then used crash-test dummies like those commonly employed by automotive companies to re-enact the impacts. Not only are the forces involved with head-to-ball impacts unlikely to cause a concussion, said the lab, but so are elbow-to-head and hand-to-head contact.

That's not to say there is no risk of getting a concussion while playing soccer. The highest risk of concussion comes from head-to-head contact, says *BJSM*. And while such contact is often accidental, *BJSM* said that in instances where such contact seems deliberate, the sport's governing body should impose very stiff penalties.

So what can a player do to reduce the risk of concussion from head-to-head contact, accidental or otherwise? Some type of headgear is the obvious answer, but the trick is to find headgear that doesn't eliminate the header from the game. A solution endorsed by FIFA and soccer players alike is the Full90 Performance Headguard, made by a company of the same name. Full90 says its headguard, a lightweight foam layer that wraps around the head, can reduce impact forces by up to 50 percent. The headguard protects crucial impact zones like the forehead, temple, and occipital (visual-processing center of the brain) areas. The design also allows the headgear to adjust to unusual head shapes like a protruding rear cranium, for example. Fortunately, the headgear has no apparent effect on the rebound speed of the ball. "It's the only product that I have ever seen that protects the player from head injury while not inhibiting performance or providing the player with an unfair advantage," says Joy Fawcett, who played for the U.S. national women's team and is an Olympic Gold Medal winner.

THE SEAL DRIBBLE

If there is one sport where an athlete can develop a signature move, it is soccer. The great Pele, for example, had his bicycle kick. Another innovation is the seal dribble of Brazilian midfielder Kerlon Souza. The move begins when Souza flicks the ball with his foot onto his head. Then, while bouncing the ball on his head like the aforementioned seal, Souza runs through the defense, who unfailingly stop his progress by fouling him, giving his team the opportunity for a free kick, preferably somewhere near the goal.

Kerlon Souza, a forward for Cruzeiro, practicing the seal dribble during team practice in Brazil in 2007.

CHAPTER 13

Swimming & Diving

HOW TO
SWIM LIKE A
CHAMPION

by MIRIAM KRAMER

This article appeared in POPULAR
MECHANICS in 2012.

IT MIGHT CONTRADICT A WIDELY USED METHOD OF TRAINING, OR IT COULD CONFIRM WHAT OLYMPIC-LEVEL COACHES HAVE KNOWN FOR YEARS, BUT EITHER WAY, NEW RESEARCH EXAMINING TWO WAYS OF SWIMMING FREESTYLE WILL MAKE A SPLASH. "TAKE YOUR MARKS." THE SWIMMERS BEND DOWN ON THEIR BLOCKS, READY. THE BUZZER SOUNDS.

Eight of the best male freestyle swimmers in the United States dive into the pool. In a little under 2 minutes the 200-meter Olympic swimming trial semifinal is over, and two swimmers are headed to the 2012 London Olympics.

Those swimmers are Michael Phelps and Ryan Lochte, two men with arguably the best freestyle form in the world. But why did Lochte beat out Phelps in this particular heat? New research being published in the *Journal of Biomechanical Engineering* may not answer that question, but it does lend a bit of scientific credence to their strokes. The short version: It's all in the arms.

Rajat Mittal is a mechanical engineer at Johns Hopkins University and lead researcher on a project to study the fastest swimming technique. Mittal says swimmers used two different kinds of arm strokes when training for and competing in freestyle events.

One, deep catch, is about as simple as swimming gets. When your arm enters the water, you try to pull it straight back exerting as much force as possible. It's a difficult stroke to master. Even the highest-level athletes need to change up their strokes on long-distance swims because of the sheer strength it takes to propel through the water with a straight arm.

The other stroke, sculling, became popular in the 1960s when a prominent coach encouraged his athletes to move their arms like propellers underwater. Instead of trying to move yourself through the water using only your shoulders, the sculling stroke allows a swimmer's elbows to jut out slightly, making it easier for the hands to wave through the water like a propeller creating less resistance.

Mittal's research focused on one seemingly simple question: Scientifically, which stroke should propel swimmers the fastest? The team started with video; USA Swimming provided Mittal and his team with underwater tapes of world-class swimmers using both the deep catch and sculling strokes while swimming laps. Mittal also modeled the arms of a few swimmers to use in computer animations of the strokes, a time-consuming process.

"It took thousands of hours for each of the simulations," Mittal says. "We had a computer cranking away for 25 or 30 days for just one result. We were trying to do comparative analysis, and analysis takes even more time and effort than the simulations."

After months of effort, Mittal and his team got their results. From a purely scientific perspective, deep catch is a far more efficient stroke. Sculling is about 20 percent less efficient than deep catch—a big number when the difference between first and last place is sometimes less than a second. The thrust created by deep catch is unmatched, Mittal says. "I think the results are somewhat controversial, but the notion that the deep catch is more effective might not be news to coaches."

Mittal's speculation seems to be spot on. Marshall Goldman, a swim coach for the Weymouth Club Waves swim team outside of Boston, who's rooting for some of his swimmers during Olympic trials this week, says these results only confirm what many coaches have known for years.

"From a swim coach's perspective, this study is an obvious thing," Goldman says. "For them to compare what they did in the 1960s to what we know about swimming these days is dumb. There have been so many different variations."

Today, most coaches want their swimmers to strive for a deeper catch on every stroke. Coaches teach three different ways of swimming freestyle: shoulder driven, core driven and hip driven. Most athletes use a combination of all three, but it depends on the event. A shoulder driven deep catch stroke can't be sustained for longer than a few hundred meters, but a hip driven hybrid of deep catch and sculling allows the swimmer to save his or her strength and finish an endurance race strong. What the research doesn't take into account, Goldman says, is that the strain put on a swimmer's shoulders by deep catch could be career shortening.

Many coaches take those concerns into account when training younger swimmers. Jim Rumbaugh, the head coach at Pilot Aquatic Club in Knoxville, Tenn., says that age plays a major role in the strokes he teaches his athletes. "It's different when you start talking about [swimmers younger than 15]," Rumbaugh says. "We typically have all of those kids using the 'S' pattern [sculling] stroke. It's easier on the joints, maintains balance, and saves the shoulders."

Mittal concedes that there's a lot more research to be done. Because this kind of computer imaging takes so long, they were only able to model and analyze the movements of one computer-simulated arm. "There are so many aspects of what makes a swimmer a swimmer that we couldn't model them all," Mittal says.

Ultimately, Mittal hopes that maybe these results will insert a little science into the way a coach picks a training method. "[This research] is not just about which one [stroke] is better than the other, but it tries to explain why one is better than the other. We used to use a coach's intuition over data, and now this will change. We have the data now."

THE GEAR OF THE 2012 GAMES

by JOE LINDSEY

When the elite compete this month at the games in London, state-of-the-art gear could mean the difference between finishing back of the pack or winning a place on the podium. These breakthroughs will help swimmers, soccer players, and triathletes go faster, higher, and stronger.

[1] **Making Waves:** Twenty-five Olympic swimming records were broken in Beijing in 2008, 23 of them by athletes wearing Speedo's LZR Racer. But the supersuit, made of a woven nylon—elastane blend with water-repellent polyurethane panels, spawned a major backlash—one coach called it a form of "technological doping." In the summer of 2009, FINA, the sport's international governing body, announced new rules for suits: textiles only (no impermeable fabrics) and no full-body coverage for men. Speedo developed a compliant LZR Racer Elite, which some athletes will wear in London, but its U.K.-based Aqualab division also got to work on the Fastskin3 System—a suit designed together with cap and goggles, marking the first time Speedo has invested heavy R&D in those accessories.

[2] **Strong Suit:** The improved hydrodynamics of the Fastskin3 Super Elite suit (above), which reduces drag up to 2.7 percent more than the LZR Racer Elite, is the result of computational fluid-dynamics analysis and water-flume tests to study passive drag (where water flows over a motionless swimmer holding a towline) and active drag (where a swimmer works at race pace). The Fastskin3 fabric—a nylon—Lycra blend—has zoned compression panels of varying densities—most knit, some woven—that help to hold the body in the most efficient position: hips high, core supported. The men's suit has a high waist, covering as much area as FINA rules allow. Exterior marker lines help athletes align the suits.

[3] **Wide View:** A lot of hydrodynamic drag comes from the head (the leading edge), especially the facial area, so Speedo used 3D head-scanning data to design goggles (opposite) that smooth out facial gaps and holes (with Western and Asian fit variants), cutting hydrodynamic drag 2.2 percent more than its Aquasocket model. A full 180-degree field of vision gives a clear view of the competition, and the lens shape significantly reduces force on the goggles, preventing them from shifting during entry and high-speed turns. Pair the new goggles with the Fastskin3 cap (opposite), whose design emerged from the same head-scanning data, and that 2.2 percent drag savings jumps to 5.7 percent.

SWIM LIKE AN OLYMPIAN

UNITED STATES
SWIMMING COACH
BOB BOWMAN MET
OLYMPIC CHAMPION
MICHAEL PHELPS
WHEN PHELPS WAS
JUST ELEVEN
YEARS OLD AND
RECOGNIZED
THE SWIMMER'S
POTENTIAL EVEN
THEN. BOWMAN
COACHED PHELPS
TO A RECORD-
SETTING 22 MEDALS
INCLUDING 18 GOLD.
IN THIS INTERVIEW
BOWMAN SAYS
SWIMMING IS
ALL ABOUT
REDUCING DRAG.

◀ Michael Phelps of the
U. S. setting a world
record in the Men's
200m Butterfly dur-
ing the 2006 Pan
Pacific Swimming
Championships in
Victoria, Canada.

WHAT'S THE MOST IMPORTANT ELEMENT IN SWIMMING?

In general, the key word is efficiency, meaning economy of
movement. You want to get the maximum distance per stroke
so you're taking the fewest number of strokes possible at the
maximum rate of speed.

HOW DO YOU DO THAT?

The number one thing is to improve the mechanics of your stroke
so that you're covering more water or more distance in a single
stroke. That's where we start. We want to build a technical model
of the stroke that has as little wasted motion as possible and
in which the underwater portion of the stroke—the propulsive
phase—is as effective as possible. We want to look at how you put
maximum pressure on the water at the right time and how you
accelerate your hand at different parts of the stroke to make the
most economical use of your resources.

WHY IS THE WAY YOU HOLD YOUR HAND IMPORTANT?

One of the things you'll see in an Olympian is that they have a
"feel for the water." It's one of those things that is very hard to
define and very easy to recognize. If you watch their hands when
they enter the water—excepting the breaststroke, of course—once
the hand is submerged, there are no air bubbles around the hand.
And that's what you want because once your hand is in the water,
you want it to be in contact with the most solid medium possible
so you get more propulsive force. If you have air bubbles under
your hand, a lot of times you're "slipping" or pushing air so you're
not as efficient. All of the great swimmers have that ability to get
their hand in the water in such a manner they won't carry air
in their hand.

IS THERE A METHOD FOR ROTATING THE HAND SO THAT ABILITY IMPROVES?

You can develop ways of entering the hand by changing the pitch
or angle of the fingers and wrist so you can maximize that.

World-record holder and Olympic champion Michael Phelps swims the breaststroke leg of the men's 200-meter individual medley during the preliminary heats at the United States Open on November 30, 2006, at the Boilermaker Aquatics Center in West Lafayette, Indiana.

IS THERE ANY PARTICULAR MOTION INVOLVED?

There are a lot of factors at play. A lot was made of the Bernoulli principle (when the velocity of a moving fluid increases, the pressure exerted by the fluid decreases, and vice versa) when swimming was revolutionized in the 1960s. There is some relevance there, but what we're finding is that swimming is more about drag force than it is about wave motion. The best freestylers in the world today put their hands in the water so they're almost pulling straight back. There is a little bit of motion sideways. It's more like a canoe paddle than it is the propeller of a boat. When you watch great swimmers like Michael Phelps or Ian Thorpe, you'll see their hands go in the water with their fingertips pointed toward the bottom so that from their fingertips up to their elbow, it basically looks like a paddle. What we tell swimmers to think about when their hands go into the water is that you want to anchor your hand on a piece of water and then apply force to move your body over your hand.

THAT'S VERY DIFFERENT THAN THE WAY IT USED TO BE.

Yes. Swimmers used to be told to make a big "S" with their arms.

WHAT PROMPTED THE CHANGE?

I think people started doing better video analysis of strokes. Swimmers like Thorpe who took quantum leaps forward in their events were naturally doing this. Phelps does it naturally. That doesn't mean there isn't a 90-degree arm bend—because there is—but that occurs when the body is moving over the hand.

WHAT ELSE CAN WE SAY ABOUT ARM AND HAND MOTION?

There should be acceleration through every stroke. Most strokes start out with an extension phase where you're trying to maximize speed gained from the last stroke cycle. So as the hand goes in the water, you apply increasing pressure so that the hand accelerates through the end of every stroke, so you build momentum for the next cycle. In every stroke, there is a propulsion phase and a recovery phase, so you want to build through the propulsion stage so that you're at maximum speed at the end. This allows you to maintain velocity while you're recovering.

WHAT'S IMPORTANT IN THE RECOVERY PHASE?

It should be as relaxed as possible and as efficient as possible. In freestyle, we want the swimmer to move his hand in a straight line forward and not out to the side where you waste motion. You want everything moving forward.

WHAT ABOUT HEAD AND NECK MOVEMENT?

One of the biggest changes in swimming that's occurred in the last six years is how we changed our thinking about what the head position should be in all the strokes. Now we want the head to be carried low as a counterbalance that allows the hips to ride higher. From the 1940s through the 1970s, the thought was that if you had your head up higher, you would ride on top of the water as if you were hydroplaning. You have to be going 35 mph to hydroplane, so that's never going to happen. So we tell swimmers to be more efficient by dropping the head lower. That creates frontal resistance on the hips so the hips are held higher. At the highest level of swimming, reducing drag is our main challenge. The challenge is not how much propulsion you can create but how much drag you can reduce because drag increases exponentially as propulsion increases. The swimmers who are most efficient at reducing drag are the best. That's the key thing in Olympic swimming.

CAP OR NO CAP?

There is no question that the cap produces less resistance than your hair even if you have your head shaved.

YOU'RE REDUCING DRAG...

... by improving body position and balance.

WHAT DO YOU DO WITH YOUR BODY?

One of the things we're focusing on is how to make your body more boat-like. What can you do to make the human body travel through the water more efficiently? Our bodies are built to move on land. But in the water, the curvature of the spine tends not to be the most efficient structure. So we have swimmers flatten their backs, elongate their necks, drop their heads, and try to be in the most rigid body position possible so that it goes through the water like a torpedo. There also is a huge focus on core strength and core stability in swimmers in every stroke.

BY CORE YOU MEAN WHAT EXACTLY?

The muscles of the abdomen and lower back. We want to make sure those muscles are involved in the stroke instead of just letting the hips do their own thing while the arms pull. They are all connected. A swimmer knows when he is losing muscle tone in his torso because his hips, arms, and shoulders are disconnected, meaning they move independently. If you maintain a tight body tone throughout your body, your whole body becomes more rigid. A high degree of body tone allows your body to move as a unit and move through the water more efficiently.

HOW IMPORTANT IS FLEXIBILITY, THEN?

Flexibility is really important because swimmers who can get into a position that makes movement through the water more fluid or easy have an advantage. Flexibility in the shoulders and the ankles is critical for getting into the most efficient position. If swimmers are tight in their shoulders, it prevents them from having a high elbow position when their hand is in front of the shoulder entering the water. If you're flexible enough to easily get into that position, you're going to have a distinct advantage over someone who has to move their body or struggle to get into that position.

HOW CRUCIAL IS THE KICK?

One area experiencing a resurgence of interest is the importance of kicking. In general, kicking is done to maintain body position. In the backstroke, of course, it is a much more propulsive force. But in long axis strokes, kicking is used much more for rhythm and maintaining body position. We place great emphasis on conditioning the legs so that they are in a state of perpetual motion during the whole swim. It's very difficult because legs have the highest level of oxygen consumption. The best swimmers are the best kickers. It gets back again to efficiency. You want to use the large muscle masses in the legs near their maximum capability and still maintain speed while avoiding lactic acid buildup.

WHAT'S THE CONNECTION BETWEEN THE STROKE AND THE KICK?

It depends on the stroke. For the butterfly, there are two distinct legs kicks per arm stroke. In the breaststroke, there is one kick per arm stroke, but that has more to do with propulsion. In freestyle, the fastest stroke is called a six-beat kick—six kicks for each stroke cycle. A stroke cycle is the stroke of both arms. Three kicks per arm.

LET'S TALK A LITTLE ABOUT AEROBIC VERSUS ANAEROBIC TRAINING.

In its purest sense, aerobic activity is exercise totally fueled by oxygen. When there is sufficient amount of oxygen in the blood, then all the energy requirements are met. In swimming, your stored energy is gone in about ten seconds and the aerobic system takes over. One of the things we do early on is to focus on aerobic training with children because while they have very little

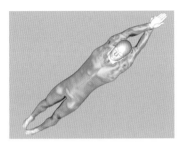

This picture highlights in yellow and orange the areas where drag affects Phelps the most.

muscle mass and very little power capability, they are very good at endurance activities. That training carries over later in their careers because many swimming events are endurance oriented. Shorter events like the 100-meter freestyle or the 50-meter freestyle are power-oriented so less time is spent on aerobic training while more time is spent on lactic-acid-type training that is anaerobic. But even the longest-distance swimmers still need that burst of speed that comes from anaerobic training. You can't really separate one from the other, but you are trying to achieve a balance between the two that is influenced by the needs of a swimmer's particular event.

WHY DOES IT SEEM AS IF SWIMMERS ARE SWIMMING FASTER ALMOST EVERY YEAR?

In recent years, it is because of improvements in underwater kicking, particularly in the freestyle, the butterfly, and the backstroke. It's the ability to go fifteen meters underwater off each wall more quickly. Swimmers have added the underwater dolphin kick motion to their repertoires, and that's what makes them faster. There are a number of drills designed to improve the underwater kick. We like to train to kick in a vertical position, with the swimmer's head out of the water and arms crossed over their chest. We time the number of kicks they can make in ten seconds. The target number is 25. That's a pretty fast rate of kicking. Once you develop a feel for doing it like that, you can start doing it through the water and accelerate off the wall.

WHAT'S SO SPECIAL ABOUT MICHAEL PHELPS AS A SWIMMER?

The thing that makes Michael better than everyone else is that he has a highly developed technical style, and he's very conscious of that all the time. He's always very efficient, and he brings that to every stroke. There is no wasted motion. He innately does this. When he swims quickly, it looks as if he isn't trying very hard. Michael learned his technique at an early age; then he got the physical training. Combine this with a great work ethic, and you have an almost unbeatable combination.

DIVING: WHEN GRAVITY MATTERS

by JEFF HUBER

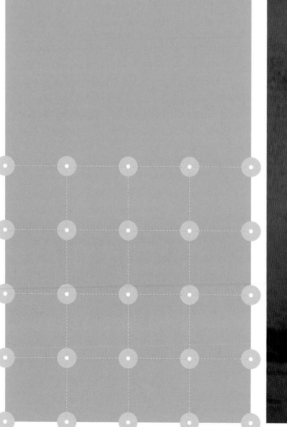

IN DIVING, 90 PERCENT OF THE SCORE COMES FROM THE DIVER'S ENTRY INTO THE WATER. BUT TO PERFORM A DIVE WELL, 90 PERCENT OF THE WORK COMES DURING THE TAKEOFF FROM THE BOARD. IN FACT, GREAT DIVES ARE OFTEN DETERMINED BEFORE THE DIVER EVEN LEAVES THE BOARD. THIS MEANS PREPARATION IS THE KEY.

◀ Greg Louganis is considered by many to be the greatest diver in history, winning two Olympic Gold Medals in 1984 and 1986, an Olympic Silver Medal in 1976, and five world championships.

DIVING TECHNIQUE

Let's imagine you're on the 3-meter springboard. Obviously, with each step of your approach, your weight presses the board down and it responds by coming back up. Timing, then, is critical. Some of the better divers know how to play the board like an instrument. You have to learn how to get it to move and be one with the board. For instance, when good divers go into their hurdle, they bend their knees for as long as possible and wait for the board to come back up to its peak so that when you drop down on the end of the board, you get the maximum amount of load. As the board comes back up, your hips are forced over the top and into the rotation.

You also want to keep the core of your body—from the waist to the shoulders—very tight because if your body loosens up, it absorbs energy. So instead of getting the most out of the board going up, you wind up getting out of position and losing energy. This energy loss often happens while swinging the arms; the arm motion tends to loosen that core because the torso is often moving as well.

The direction of your flight is determined by the position of your ankles and your center of gravity on the end of the board. The two points—your ankle position and your center of gravity—determine the vector or direction your body will actually take. Position will sometimes vary according to the type of dive being performed.

Speed of rotation is determined by the amount of force used during takeoff. Speed of rotation is also affected by the tightness or compactness of the tuck, pike, or twist position. The tighter the tuck or pike position, the greater the speed of rotation around the horizontal axis. For the pike position, for example, a diver needs to get into a compact pike and get as flat as possible. Coaches don't want to see any daylight between the torso and legs once divers flatten their stomachs onto their legs.

BODY-POSITIONING PROBLEMS

Among less proficient divers, the tuck or pike position tends to open up as centrifugal force pulls it apart. When that happens, it is really difficult to finish a dive because you are out of position and you can't control it. You also want to be tight or compact along the vertical axis when you're twisting during the dive. You want to pull as tight as possible in order to get a very rapid twist. Keeping the body straight allows it to turn as a single entity. If your body core is soft, then when the shoulders twist the hips won't turn with them. That's when the legs start to come apart and very little twisting occurs. The better divers are able to pull in tight and actually increase the speed of the rotation along the vertical axis. During the twisting motion, the dive actually becomes slightly tilted along the vertical axis, which requires the diver to bring one hand up and the other hand down and then pull both arms to a T position. This motion coming out of the twist brings the body position back in line with the vertical axis and allows the diver to line up straight going into the water without any casting of the body. A cast on the entry would throw water toward the judges and cause the entry to be less "clean" going through the water and thereby cause a deduction in the score.

RELATION TO THE ENVIRONMENT

Height off the board is a key ingredient of a successful dive. Studies have shown that even if your rotation is a little slow but you have a good "top," you'll do a good dive. If you have good height, it means you were in the right position and on the right vector. Good height also means you're going to have a lot more time to come out of the dive and get your hands lined up to "rip" the dive.

The "rip" has to do with the sound the diver makes going through the water. It almost sounds like someone ripping paper. Think of the water as a piece of paper that you approach with your hands held together. As you come into contact with it, you try to tear or rip apart the paper so that you can go through it. Some divers are so good at making a clean entry that it looks as if they've displaced just two teaspoons of water upon entry, which, of course, is the purpose of the rip entry: to not make a splash. The sound, however, can be quite impressive and can influence a judge's score.

Once in the water, there is still some time for correction if necessary. Once underwater, divers routinely pull their hands down to their hips in a swimming motion that creates air pockets around the diver. If, however, the diver's feet are moving past vertical, a diver may do a "save" by bending at the waist and pushing the feet back in the opposite direction, or conversely, do a "scoop" by pulling the head back and doing a half-somersault underwater. That's been done on dives scored as perfect.

When Mark Lenzi won the Olympic Gold Medal in Barcelona in 1992, he probably wasn't the best diver at that meet, but he was the best prepared in terms of executing his takeoffs and entries. Lenzi also benefited from an uncanny ability to know where his body was at all times during a dive. Most divers count the number of taps made by the board after they've launched, to orient themselves.

Good divers are often blessed with the ability to pick up on audible or visual cues during the course of their dive. They know where they are spatially even when they are upside down. The great diver Greg Louganis told me he could hear how close he was to the water by the sound of the water sprayer used to prevent the surface of the water from becoming glassy (which affects depth perception). Other divers say they count the number of taps made by the board after they've launched off it. Olympic champion Mark Lenzi had an uncanny ability to know where his body was at all times during a dive.

Related to this cue recognition is the ability to control arousal levels. We know that when arousal levels go up, cue utilization tends to go down. A certain amount of emotional intensity can increase alertness, but at a certain point athletes get tunnel vision and they don't see their spots. So when it's time to do the big dive and win the meet, they miss their spots. I've seen kids who get so fired up that they can't control their motor movements.

Recognizing that you will miss your spots if you get too excited or anxious is half the battle. The next step is learning mental strategies such as monitoring breathing or performing physical routines that remind you to stay relaxed. At the Olympic level, the people who do the best job of that perform very well. Interestingly, 99 percent of an athlete's performance is mental, even though we spend 99 percent of our time on the physical training. That's probably because it's easier to emphasize training the body than it is to get into someone's head. We spend a lot of years perfecting performance, but there is more to it than that. As an athlete, you need to buy into the fact that there is an inner game. It's a lot of work, but the great ones buy into that and understand it. In a sense, we have to be attuned to the physics of diving but also to the metaphysics of diving!

CHAPTER 14

Tennis

POWER
SERVE

by STEVE FLINK

MANY MATCHES PLAYED IN MEN'S PROFESSIONAL TENNIS ARE ESSENTIALLY EXERCISES IN BRUTALITY, FEATURING EXPLOSIVE POWER ALMOST ACROSS THE BOARD. THIS GENERATION OF COMBATANTS IS STRONG AND DURABLE, CAPABLE OF BLASTING THE OPPOSITION OFF THE COURT WITH THE EXTRAORDINARY PACE OF ITS SHOT-MAKING, AND IS ABLE TO PRODUCE BLINDING WINNERS FROM ALMOST ANYWHERE ON THE COURT.

Rafael Nadal, the "King of Clay," serves a ball to Novak Djokovic during the final of the AFP Rome Tennis Masters on May 21, 2012.

While power prevails throughout the competitive game of tennis, it is most evident, and probably of greatest significance, on the serve. With one swing of the racket, the server can begin and end a point abruptly, keeping a rival completely off guard with the speed, spin, and placement of his delivery. The most potent servers enjoy an immense advantage over those who cannot produce the same degree of pace. The ability to generate an enormous amount of speed on the serve translates into free points, intimidates those on the receiving end who have trouble coming to terms with the high velocity, and provides a cushion in the heat of a long battle.

Big servers dominate today's game. The best players in the sport use the strength of their serve as their primary weapon. The most striking example of a champion coming into prominence in large measure because of his big serve is Pete Sampras, who was inducted into the Tennis Hall of Fame in 2007.

THE LEGENDARY SAMPRAS

Sampras demoralized more than his share of opponents with his devastating first serve, keeping them constantly guessing about where he was going with it, moving it around skillfully from corner to corner. Sampras epitomizes the modern men's champion, building his game around the explosive serve, pulling away from capable foes with the effortless ferocity of his delivery. That astonishing first serve was frequently clocked at 120–140 mph. This velocity occurs in a relatively small space when you consider that the court measures 78 feet in length and 27 feet in width for singles' tennis. The serve operates within even tighter dimensions in that the distance from the server to the opposite service line is about 60 feet.

Sampras and other stupendous servers such as Boris Becker and Goran Ivanisevic won about 80 percent of all points when they got their first serve in play. That ratio of success is a direct result of power. But where does the power come from on the serve? How do the best of the breed create such remarkable velocity with regularity?

To be sure, there are common components shared by all of the great servers, even if techniques vary among competitors. As Allen Fox, former American Davis Cup player and former tennis coach at Pepperdine University, explains, there are "three or four" sources of power that are used by players who know what they're doing.

"The object is to get the racket head moving as fast as you possibly can," says Fox. "It is done like a linear accelerator. You keep adding boosts of power from various sources until you get the ultimate racket velocity. That comes from bending your knees, throwing the racket head over your shoulder, and rotating your shoulders. That adds to the speed already coming from your legs and torso. Then you snap your wrist. Add all of those elements together, and that is where you get your power."

Australian Colin Dibley, a teaching professional in New Jersey, had the biggest serve of his era when he played the circuit in the 1970s. He describes the basis for power similarly to Fox, but adds a few of his own comments to the equation.

"You've got to use your whole body," says Dibley. "I know from my own experience that if I try to hit the serve too hard, I can lose it all. It is a matter of timing and balance. You have to transfer your weight into the ball. Players often get their weight forward too soon, and they end up hitting only with their arm."

Dibley emphasizes the importance of a good ball toss in developing a forceful serve. "To get power," he says, "you always have to go up after the ball. Wherever you toss the ball, you have to make sure you are extending up after the ball. A lot of club players toss too high and let the ball drop too low, or they don't throw the ball high enough, and therefore don't extend for power."

THE BALL TOSS

To get maximum power on the serve, the player must toss the ball out in front of his body, but not too far forward. "The ball should ideally bounce six to nine inches in front of your body if you were to let the toss drop to the ground rather than making contact with the ball," notes Dibley. "If you toss too far out in front of your body, you will be at the end of your reach and will get too much arm and very little else into the serve. But if you can meet the ball at the peak of the toss—or somewhere near the top of the toss—and place the ball slightly in front of your body, then you will get the most power."

The consistency and placement of the toss will determine the direction and pace of the serve. According to studies done by the

Steffi Graf demonstrating an unusually high toss. This has caused her trouble when the ball was blown around by the wind.

Vic Braden Tennis College in Cota de Caza, California, the ideal toss should be seventeen to twenty inches above the racket hand, at what is called the "peak of the reach."

Of course, the top players toss the ball the way it works for them. Steffi Graf, widely acknowledged as one of the best and biggest servers in women's tennis, had an unusually high toss, which caused her considerable trouble when the ball was blown around by the wind. Ivan Lendl had another uncommonly high toss, although he altered it over the years to make it lower.

Despite the disparity in their tosses, all servers share something more significant. No matter how high or low they make their tosses, they place the ball in the same place time after time, point after point, and therefore they get not only power but consistency as a reward for their discipline and effort. Furthermore, those who excel in the serving department share another trait that is not related to the toss—a relaxed serving arm.

THE SERVING ARM

"The arm has to be loose," confirms Fox, "because it is essentially a passive element. The arm is accelerated by the shoulders, the legs, and the torso. The arm simply allows these accelerators to work without resisting it. If the arm is stiff and you try to muscle the serve, you might actually lose power. Sampras was very loose in his arm when he served."

RACKET TECHNOLOGY

Has racket technology had anything to do with the proliferation of big serving in the modern game? The single advancement most responsible for today's blindingly fast serves, says Rod Cross, a physicist at Australia's University of Sydney, is the oversize racket head. The game was transformed as the hitting surface of rackets grew to the current legal limit of 15.5 by 11.5 inches—established in 1981. "Players hit the ball as hard as they can, and give it enough topspin to make it land in the court," Cross says. "You couldn't do that with a small wooden racket—the ball would have clipped the frame."

As Fox says, "The velocity of the serve comes from how fast the racket is moving at contact and how energy is transferred to the ball. The new rackets probably move at the same speed as older ones, but there is greater energy transfer to the ball with the newer rackets. The wide-body is stiffer. In the old days, the racket flexed backward and then the ball left before it flexed forward. Therefore, the energy was wasted in flexing the racket. These new rackets don't flex as much, so more energy is transferred to the ball."

Ram Ramnath, Ph.D., professor of aeronautics at MIT and technical advisor for the ATP tour, makes an important point when
he talks about how the changing sweet spot relates to the fast-paced serving in the game today. "With the newer rackets," he points out, "the sweet spot is being raised all the time." Companies like Wilson are trying to make the sweet spot higher on the racket's strings. For very good servers, the high sweet spot, combined with the high speed of the racket, can result in great power. They make contact with the ball slightly higher on the strings for maximum power.

The most recent development in rackets relates to weight. The conventional weight of most rackets until now has been 12.4 ounces, but the trend in some of the newer wide-body frames is to make them about 10% lighter, or ten ounces. If these lighter rackets are balanced properly, they have the capacity to contribute to a larger sweet spot—a movement that could only be a positive step for the power server.

THE SERVE RECEIVER

The advancements in rackets are benefiting players in other aspects of the game. There may well be more great power servers around than ever before, but on the other side of the net is the rapidly growing number of players who can return serves with increasing effectiveness.

Fox presents an interesting point of view on the topic. "I would have to say," he begins, "that the big servers do not enjoy as much of an advantage as they used to have. It used to be worse for the receiver. Fred Stolle would play John Newcomb in the 1960s and there would be no points to watch. The server in matches like the Stolle-Newcomb battles was dominant in a way I haven't seen since. The counterattacker gets a fair shake today because there are few grass-court tournaments and the ball is heavier than it used to be."

Clearly, the serve will remain a critical weapon across the entire spectrum of the men's game, and it has taken on increasing value among the women as well. For example, Venus Williams delivered a record-breaking serve of 129 mph in 2007.

WOMEN POWER UP

With more female players becoming taller and stronger, the power serve is now just as big a part of the women's game as it is in the men's. Venus Williams, for example, is 6-foot-1, while 1970s and 1980s star Chris Evert is 5-foot-6. In June 2005, only one of the top ten women's players was under 5-foot-8$\frac{1}{2}$, with the average being 5-foot-10.

Venus Williams of the U.S. serves against Vera Douchevina of Russia during day four of the Australian Open Grand Slam at Melbourne Park on January 22, 2004.

ANATOMY OF
A SERVE

by TOM COLLIGAN

ANDY RODDICK, WHO RETIRED IN 2012, ONCE HAD THE WORLD'S FASTEST TENNIS SERVE—HIS 155-MPH SCORCHER IN 2004 SET A RECORD—BUT HE DIDN'T LIKE TO TALK ABOUT IT. WHEN HE FIRST MET PATRICK McENROE, HIS DAVIS CUP COACH, HE SAID: "WHATEVER YOU DO, DON'T SAY ANYTHING TO ME ABOUT MY SERVE. IF I THINK ABOUT IT, I'M IN TROUBLE." HERE'S WHAT REALLY HAPPENS IN THE TWO-THIRDS OF A SECOND BETWEEN TOSS AND ACE.

Roger Federer from Switzerland serves the ball to his Serbian opponent, Novak Djokovic, during the final match of the Montreal Masters tennis tournament in Montreal, Canada, in August 2007. Djokovic won 7–6 (7–2), 2–6, and 7–6 (7–2) in this upset victory against the top seed Federer.

THE WINDUP

As the toss goes up, players press their feet against the court, using ground reaction forces to build up elastic potential energy—rotations of the legs, hips, trunk, and shoulders that produce maximum angular momentum. Exploding upward toward the ball, pro players employ extraordinary timing to efficiently transfer forces from the legs, through the body segments, to the striking hand in what biomechanists call "the kinetic chain principle." Bruce Elliott, a professor at the University of Western Australia, has extrapolated the contributions of the body segments to racket-head speed (shown on next page) using 3-D videography and computer analysis. "These contributions vary from person to person," Elliott says, "but the data shows the clear importance of the trunk, shoulder internal rotation, and wrist flexion in the swing to impact."

UPPER ARM 10%

RACKET-HEAD SPEED 100%

LEGS AND TRUNK 20%

FOREARM 40%

HAND 30%

THE TOSS

A high, confident toss made 1 to 2 feet inside the baseline allows the server to uncoil both upward and forward into the court, making contact at 1.5 times body height. For Roddick, at 6-foot-2, that is roughly 9.5 feet off the ground.

A pro player looks for variations in height or location of his opponent's tosses to predict where the serve is headed—and adjusts accordingly. Top servers, however, give away nothing. "Andy can hit it hard to different corners with the same toss," McEnroe says. "Players just can't pick it up."

THE STRIKE

On a 120-mph serve, the ball is in contact with the racket strings for about five milliseconds, moving up to five inches laterally across the string plane, gathering spin. The tip of the racket moves at nearly 120 mph, though at the point of impact, a few inches closer to the ground, the racket is moving roughly 22 percent slower. The ball's additional speed comes from both the elastic energy in the rubber, which returns 53 to 58 percent of the force exerted upon it, and the racket strings (strung at an average of 60 pounds of tension), which stretch about one inch during the impact.

ACCEPTANCE WINDOW

As the ball rockets off the strings, it must travel within a very narrow range of angles to both clear the net and bounce inside the service box. Coaches call this tiny wedge of potential trajectories the "acceptance window." It shrinks as the serve goes faster—requiring incredible timing and precision to deliver a 120-mph serve inbounds. There are, however, things that the server can do (short of hitting the ball more slowly) to increase the size of the acceptance window. University of Pennsylvania physics Professor Howard Brody has identified two key tactics: strike the ball as high off the ground as possible or give the ball more topspin, which creates an area of low pressure beneath the ball (the phenomenon known as the Magnus effect) to make it nose-dive into the service court.

SPIN

A tennis ball's spin barely decreases during flight, and it actually increases when the ball hits the court. "Looking at slow-motion video, you can see that the friction of the court grabs the bottom of the ball, while the top continues to rotate, adding more spin, and converting sidespin into almost pure topspin," says videographer and tennis instructor John Yandell. The average 2,400-rpm spin rate that Yandell has observed in Roddick's 130-mph serves doubles after the ball hits the court's surface—to a whopping 4,800 rpm. This creates the "heavy ball" effect—a shot with so much movement and spin that opponents feel as though they're returning a shot put.

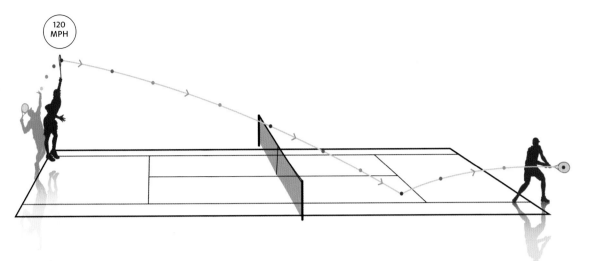

VELOCITY

The serve speeds you see on courtside digital displays are measured just as the ball leaves the racket. Fortunately for returners, by the time the ball reaches them, air resistance and the friction of the court surface have diminished its speed by roughly 50 percent. Yandell has found that, on average, a 120-mph serve slows to 82 mph before the bounce, then to 65 mph after the bounce, and finally to 55 mph at the opponent's racket.

FIRST AND SECOND SERVES

Pros are successful on 50 to 60 percent of their first serves, which are faster and have flatter trajectories than their second, slower serves. At the 2007 Wimbledon tournament, Roddick nailed a 133-mph first serve (blue) that hit the court hard and bounced low with slice—sidespin that curves and draws the returner wide of the sideline.

On a second serve (yellow), Roddick employed a 102-mph "kick serve" with heavy topspin, created by brushing the strings upward against the back of the ball. This made the serve dive into the box, and it generated a high bounce that was difficult to return. First serves are flashy, but second serves are a better predictor of success: The top three players in the world are men who've won the most points on their second serve.

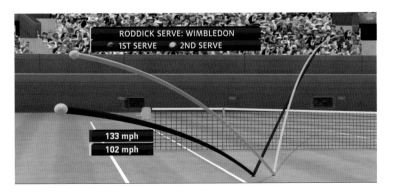

RODDICK SERVE: WIMBLEDON
1ST SERVE   2ND SERVE
133 mph
102 mph

ANATOMY OF A SERVE   241

REVERSE FOREHAND

The reverse forehand stroke was popularized by Pete Sampras and has since been picked up by many players. This is a stroke allows a player to hit cross-court without hitting long, even though he is late to the ball. The reverse forehand starts with a strong hit with your arm extended up and behind you. But instead of hitting across the front of your body, you bring the racket back up in "reverse." The racket should end above where it started.

STRING THEORY

While the last 35 years have seen major modifications in rackets and the materials used to make them, the same revolution is occurring in the material that goes in them. Tennis rackets have traditionally been strung with gut, a natural material made from part of the intestines of cows. But now strings are made from synthetic materials such as nylon and polyester.

Synthetic strings first attracted attention in 1997 when an unseeded Brazilian player, Gustavo Kuerten, won the first of three French Opens using Luxilon synthetic strings. Soon other players made the switch—sometimes opting for a hybrid of synthetic and gut before making the switch to synthetic strings entirely. The synthetic strings let players take bigger cuts at the ball without sacrificing control. Players maintain that the synthetic strings allow them to put more topspin on the ball, so the ball stays in play despite the huge velocities generated by powerful swings. Lastly, the synthetic strings are more durable than gut.

Critics note that synthetic strings make it harder to volley and attribute the decline of serve-and-volley specialists in the game to their increased use.

THE PHYSICS OF TENNIS RACKET STRINGS

by ALLEN ST. JOHN

TODAY'S HIGH-TECH STRINGING HELPS KEEP TENNIS PROS UNDER CONTROL. WHEN WATCHING THE PROS AT THE U.S. OPEN HIT WITH SUPERHUMAN PACE, IT'S NATURAL TO LOOK FOR A SHORTCUT TO ATTAIN THAT KIND OF POWER. MOST WEEKEND HACKERS MIGHT FOCUS ON THE RACKET, ASSUMING THAT IF THEY COULD DIP INTO A TOP PRO'S RACKET BAG, THEY TOO COULD PUMMEL THE BALL LIKE A PRO.

Novak Djokovic serves to Roger Federer during the Australian Open Tennis Championship semi-finals in Melbourne, Australia, on January 27, 2011.

They may be only part right. In 2010, defending champion Roger Federer used a frame that is a direct descendent of the racket used by Pete Sampras—a small-head, low-power model introduced way back in 1982. But conventional frames like his contain a secret weapon: specialized, high-tech string. So, it's not the frame, but it may be the string.

Pros are more particular about their string jobs than about their post-match massages.

"They have their rackets in their hands hours and hours every day," says Roman Prokes, president of PRNY Tennis in New York and personal stringer to stars like Maria Sharapova and Andy Roddick. "So if you mess it up by a pound of tension, they know it." Or in the words of Andre Agassi, one of Prokes' most famous clients: "A string job can be the difference in a match. A match can be the difference in a career. And a career can mean the difference in countless lives."

What do they string with? Most pros are using polyester from Luxilon or other companies. The small Belgian company also makes elastics for bras and other women's undergarments. Its climb to fame began when a young Brazilian player named Gustavo Kuerten tried the then-obscure string, almost on a whim, and won three French Opens with it. Other players gradually followed suit, and now virtually every player on the men's and women's tour who runs the stringing room at the U.S. Open uses Luxilon or a Luxilon play-alike.

The polyester string is both stiffer and thicker than conventional gut and nylon strings, and the result is a unique set of playing characteristics. "Polyester strings grab the ball—it's almost like suction cups," says Prokes, who oversees the stringing room at the U.S. Open. It will churn out more than 3,000 string jobs over the course of the fortnight.

Why do players love Luxilon? In a word: "Control," Prokes says. And in modern tennis, control means topspin. Topspin is the forward rotation of the ball, imparted by an exaggerated low-to-high swing. The forward rotation disrupts air pressure around the ball, creating a zone of high pressure above the ball and low pressure below—the same forces that are at work on a bat-breaking baseball pitch. This unequal pressure forces the ball to dip down, allowing players to swing hard, aim higher over the net and still land the ball inside the baseline. "You can hit the ball hard and it stays in the court," Prokes says.

This extreme spin from polyester-strung rackets also allows players to hit angles that simply aren't possible with conventional string. Topspin also gives players a secondary advantage in that the spin makes the ball bounce higher, forcing opponents to hit the ball at shoulder height, out of their comfort zone.

The dramatic difference in spin isn't subtle. Tennis researcher John Yandell analyzed slow-motion video and determined that Rafael Nadal hits his average forehand with 3,200 rotations per minute (rpm) and sometimes reaches a mind-boggling 4,900 rpm. By comparison, Federer's forehand averages 2,700. And Pete Sampras and Andre Agassi, two of the top players of the previous generation, hit their forehand at a mere 1,800 rpm, imparting slightly more than half as much spin as Nadal.

While the next generation of strings have taken the pro game by storm, they're not a panacea for the recreational player. They require a full, fast swing to create the spin, and the stiff string bed causes vibrations that can aggravate tennis elbow.

Albeit minor, the downside of polyester strings is that they lose their tension quickly. And pros are particular about their string tension. To maintain a consistent tension throughout the match, Federer started the trend of changing rackets at predetermined intervals, usually every eight games with each ball change. Most top players have followed suit.

Many pros will have all their rackets restrung every night whether they played with them or not. Overnight, Prokes explains, rackets will lose a pound to a pound and a half of tension, and that's enough to put it outside the margin for error. Players can detect differences of a half-pound of tension or less just by tapping a racket against the palm. "To them that's the difference between the ball flying and it doesn't."

Most players will carry a small arsenal of rackets strung at a narrow range of tensions so they can grab a slightly different racket if the conditions change or they need a little more power or control. Prokes explains that he had strung rackets at three different tensions—58 pounds, 59 pounds and 60 pounds— for Andy Roddick's first-round match, increasing the tension slightly to help control the lively ball under hot conditions. Top-seeded Nadal is the exception to this array-of-rackets rule. All of his Babolat frames are strung at exactly the same tension—56 pounds—and he makes the adjustments in his game depending on the conditions. "In a way, he adjusts to the string," Prokes says.

PHOTOGRAPHY CREDITS

INDEX

HEARST BOOKS
New York

An Imprint of Sterling Publishing
387 Park Avenue South
New York, NY 10016

Portions of this book have previously appeared in
How a Curveball Curves, 978-1-58816-475-9

Book Design: Agustin Chung

ISBN 978-1-61837-122-5

Distributed in Canada by Sterling Publishing
℅ Canadian Manda Group, 165 Dufferin Street
Toronto, Ontario, Canada M6K 3H6
Distributed in the United Kingdom by GMC Distribution Services
Castle Place, 166 High Street, Lewes, East Sussex, England BN7 1XU
Distributed in Australia by Capricorn Link (Australia) Pty. Ltd.
P.O. Box 704, Windsor, NSW 2756, Australia

For information about custom editions, special sales, and premium and
corporate purchases, please contact Sterling Special Sales at
800-805-5489 or specialsales@sterlingpublishing.com.

Manufactured in China

4 6 8 10 9 7 5

www.sterlingpublishing.com